IMAGES
of America

LATINOS
IN PASADENA

D1601983

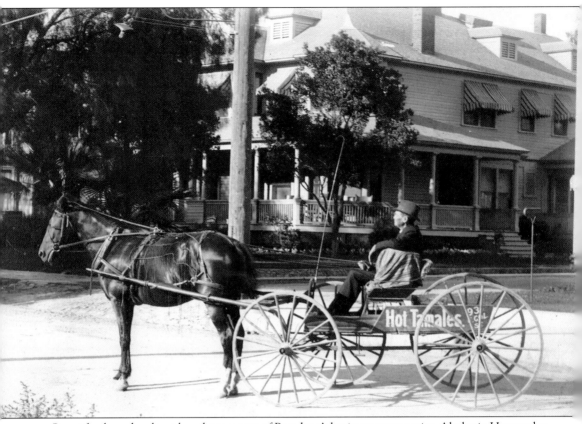

Street food vendors have long been a part of Pasadena's business community. Abalenio Hernandez is listed in the 1910 census as living at 615 South Broadway, Pasadena, with his wife, Rita. He is 50 years old in the picture and immigrated to the United States in 1895. One has to wonder if Rita was the silent partner who made the tamales. (Pasadena Museum of History.)

IMAGES
of America

LATINOS
IN PASADENA

Roberta H. Martínez

ARCADIA
PUBLISHING

Published by Arcadia Publishing
Charleston SC, Chicago IL, Portsmouth NH, San Francisco CA

Printed in the United States of America

Library of Congress Control Number: 2009921001

For all general information contact Arcadia Publishing at:
Telephone 843-853-2070
Fax 843-853-0044
E-mail sales@arcadiapublishing.com
For customer service and orders:
Toll-Free 1-888-313-2665

Visit us on the Internet at www.arcadiapublishing.com

To my grandpa Cesareo Villa and my parents, Nellie and Pete Martínez, whose music and stories fed my mind and filled my soul.

CONTENTS

ACKNOWLEDGMENTS

I thank: Yuny Parada, who offered guidance and images and told me I *must* write this book, then helped me throughout; Daisy Chilin for her assistance in whatever task was necessary; and Inez Yslas, who helped with technical coordination and phone calls. The following individuals shared knowledge and their life experiences: Paul Ayers, Stacy Camp, Dr. Daniel Castro, Don Chaput, Lisa Derderian, Dr. Lynne Emery, Juanita Espino, Serafin Espinoza, Delfina Esquivel, Daniel Estrada, Vanessa Flores, Elias Galvan, Catherine Haskett Hany, Michael Heralda, Lilia Hernández, Maria Luisa Isenberg, Steve Lamb, firefighter Victor Laveaga, Abel Lopez, Lorraine Lopez, Felipe Agredano Lozano, Michaela Mares, Ed Maya, Gregory McReynolds, Roger Mejia, Robert Monzon, Elizabeth Pomeroy, Janet Pope-Givens, Abel Ramirez, Joe Robledo, Julie Chavez Rodriguez, Nicholas Rodriguez, Raul R. Rodriguez, Dave Ruiz, Paul Secord, Belen Lopez Segura, Capt. Dan Serna of the Pasadena Fire Department, Bruce Smith, Luis Torres, Chester King User, Mauricio Valadez, Maxine Garcia Wardell, and Marge Wyatt.

I also want to thank Gamble House director Ted Bosley; Huntington Library's Jennifer Watts and Erin Chase; Los Encinos State Historical Park's Michael Crosby; Pasadena Museum of History's Jeannette O'Malley, as well as Laura Verlaque and Kirk Meyers, Bob Bennett, Sid Gally, George Hiyakawa, Julie Stires, and Carol Watson; Pasadena Police Department's acting chief, Christopher Vicino, as well as officer Victor Cass and Susana Castro; Pasadena Public Library's Jan Sanders and executive director Dan Mclaughlin; Kelly Sutherlin McLeod and Michelle Rueda; Institute for the Study of the American West, including Marva Felchlin, Kim Walters, and Liza Posas; and University of Southern California Digital Archives' Los Angeles and Southern California History and Special Collections, particularly Dace Taub and Rachelle Balinas Smith. Thanks must go to the scholarly work and previous volumes by Francisco Balderrama, William Deverell, Marguerite Duncan-Abrams, Michael James, Robert H. Peterson, Manuel Pineda, Ann Scheid, and Michelle Zack.

Special appreciation goes to Ed and Rita Almanza, Brian Biery at www.brianbiery.com, James M. Grimes and Mark Humphrey at www.humphreyphotography.com, and J. Michael Walker at www.jmichaelwalker.com for image use.

Pat and Rosalina Guerrero and Yvonne Ruiz deserve special thanks for working well out of the limelight because they believed stories must be shared. A special thanks to the members of the Pasadena Mexican American History Association, who shared their life stories, trusting that we would honor their gift. On a very personal note, I want to thank the kiddoes near and far, Matt, Kate, Matthew, Lili, and Celi, for loving me and respecting my work. And finally, thanks to the love of my life, James Grimes, who is always there with his advice, grammatical opinion, and love.

INTRODUCTION

Every place has a history, and every community has stories that define its character, sometimes from multiple perspectives that conflict and coexist simultaneously. Sometimes the story of a place can be told within a very local focus, and sometimes the history's roots and branches connect to foreign governments and ancestral lands. The history of Latinos in Pasadena is in the second category. The history of the city of Pasadena is one of migrants and immigrants. Early settlers arrived from Spain and other countries via Mexico in the 18th century. Others came from the eastern and southern portions of the United States in the 19th and 20th centuries. Yet others have arrived from countries in Central and South America, the Caribbean, and the Philippines in each of these centuries. A common phrase describing the heritage of the Hispanic or Latino mentions the *tres raices,* or three roots, meaning the ancestral roots from Africa, Europe, and the indigenous peoples. Living on the West Coast, we need to add a fourth root, Asia. Within the history of Latinos in Pasadena is a microcosm of the Latino experience nationwide. We are members of the community whose families were in this area as the city of Pasadena began and of those who will arrive after this book is printed.

There are those who would only wish to be referred to as Chicano, Hispanic, Americans of Latin or Mexican descent, and those who don't care what you call them, as long as you are respectful. In general, I have chosen to use the word Latino to describe the greater community because our history has included many groups with multiple immigrant generations. Others might have chosen otherwise; I respect their personal choice as I hope they respect mine. Throughout the history of the area though, the bulk of the Latinos have had a tie with Mexico. They have historically been the group with the largest numbers. In the last two decades, the demographics have changed and while Mexicans are still the bulk of the community, Latinos with roots in other countries have increased in number.

Currently, nearly 30 percent of those with Spanish surnames and registered to vote are Republican, and the rest are Democrats, Green, and Independent. Some are straight and some are gay. Some have an education and world experience that rival diplomats, while some have never traveled as far as the Arroyo Seco. Some live in a part of the community where they are surrounded by Spanish only, others by English only, and yet others who are comfortable in both, occasionally switching mid-sentence to the words that better express their point. This "code-switching" is common among those who are comfortable with, or fluent in, more than one language. The sum of these reflects the experience and identity of Latinos in Pasadena. There will be some code-switching in the book, but it will be minimal.

The complexity of community and individual identity is an integral theme; how we view ourselves and how others view us is a common thread throughout. As a person who grew up in East Los Angeles and with academic training in history, I lived in Pasadena for 15 years and had no idea of the size of the Latino community or of its role in Pasadena history. Because the history of the Latino community is not well known, there is a need for establishing the context in which events took place. The first chapter of the book tells something of the *raices*, or roots, of the Latino community in Pasadena. The rest of the book focuses on the *ramas*, or branches, that developed and eventually flourished as the community grew.

I chose not to cover topics that receive large amounts of press or that could best be served by experts in a specialized field. Because ink and space are finite, the focus is on what might not be found easily elsewhere. As writer and reader, we are indebted to the Pasadena Mexican American History Association. Led by Manny Contreras, they have held on to images and stories that informed much of the writing of this book. In 1997, they presented an "exhibit of photographs displaying early Pasadena . . . with the help and/or contributions of rare photographs by the following individuals or groups: Carmel Meza Collection, Mary Ann Montañez Collection, Maxine Garcia Wordell Collection, Mijares Restaurant Collection, Memorabilia of Pasadena Booklets, Pasadena Mexican-American History Association, Uni-Vets Club of Pasadena, and numerous volunteers." This book could be seen as an extension of that effort. Hopefully volumes will follow; there still is so much more to be shared.

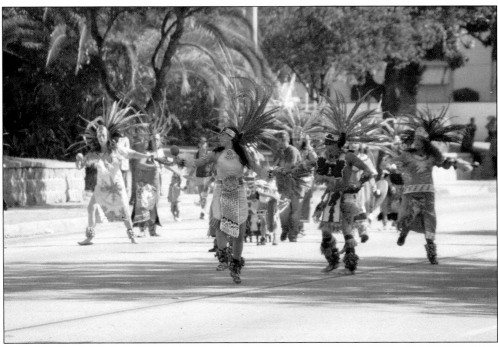

Danza Yankuitlitl, which means "new fire," is directed by Maestra Margarita Calderon and is a group based in Pasadena. The group performs Mexican indigenous dances—the *danzantes* share these dances with the community at large to develop friendship and understanding through the sharing of culture and dance. El Es Dios is an expression of reverence shared before they begin their danza. (Latino Heritage Collection.)

One

RAICES Y RAMAS

In 1492, King Ferdinand and Queen Isabella of Spain made an effort, in concert with the Spanish Inquisition, to consolidate their kingdom, establish colonies, and convert their subjects to Roman Catholicism. The era of the acceptance of multiple religions—Muslim, Catholic, and Jew—in the Iberian Peninsula had ended. Those who left Spain represented the religious and cultural communities that had lived together for five centuries and had preceded Ferdinand and Isabella's ascendancy. Colonizing Nueva España was of paramount importance. Pedro Alonso Niño, of African heritage, served as navigator for Christopher Columbus. For the next three centuries, colonies were established and the social system that developed was complex, based on geographic origin, socioeconomics, and the ethnic lineage of parents. There were as many as 16 different social stations or castas. *Penisulares*, those born on the Iberian Peninsula, were most powerful. *Criollos*, born in America, their parents born in Spain, could not attain the same level of position because of their place of birth. Casta paintings visually expressed these distinctions. They served as both news service and social delineators, clearly defining position and status. There were many unions that existed in Latin America; the mestizos, of Spanish and Mesoamerican heritage, and the mulatto, of Spanish and African heritage, were most common. Many Africans were brought as slaves from Africa, the earliest recorded in the 16th century. The incursion of the Spanish into *Maya* and *Mexica* territories were also a part of this era. While this was taking place in Nueva España, the Tongva of what is now Southern California lived in clans and settlements, trading among themselves and others, from what we know as the San Gabriel Mountains to Catalina Island. Sufficiency and sustainability were maintained by group size and knowledge of animal, land, and sea. Chants, dance, drawings, and songs were a part of the culture that was shared by those appointed as culture bearers.

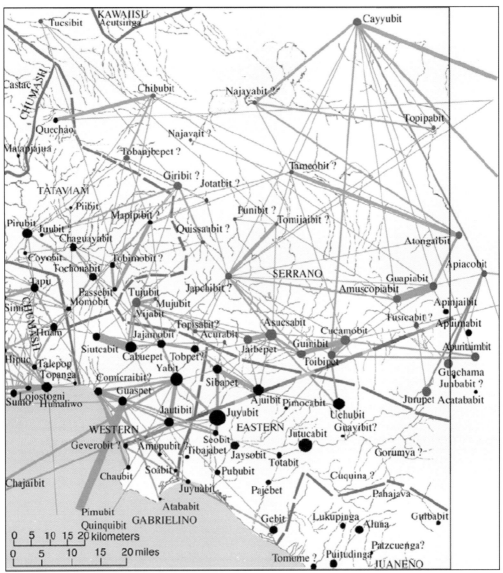

The Tongva lived in as many as 30 to 40 areas in the San Gabriel and San Fernando Valleys. Their work and roles were based primarily along gender lines: women gathered and cooked, and men fished and hunted. Each worked on tasks that supported their main work—basket weaving for women, net-working for men. They traveled by foot or by *ti'ats* (canoes). According to Dr. Rosanne Welch, those who were most successful as artisans, hunters, or traders were at the top of the hierarchical structure. Families of long lineage, of past contribution to the tribe, were at the next level. The third group was the remainder of the population. Chiefs, based on blood lineage, could be male or female. Primary sources for our knowledge of their culture were Bartolomea de Comcrabit and Narcissas Higuera, both Tongva. With the establishment of the missions, many natives were absorbed or enveloped by the culture of *Nueva España*. Nearly 6,000 Tongva lie buried in the grounds of the Misión San Gabriel. Among those buried may be Prospero, who was at the mission in 1804. He was given, or took, the last name Dominguez. With the secularization of lands, records were lost or not kept. Members of the Tongva nation are currently investigating and reconstructing their culture and searching for relatives who were absorbed into the society of Nueva España. (Chester King User.)

10

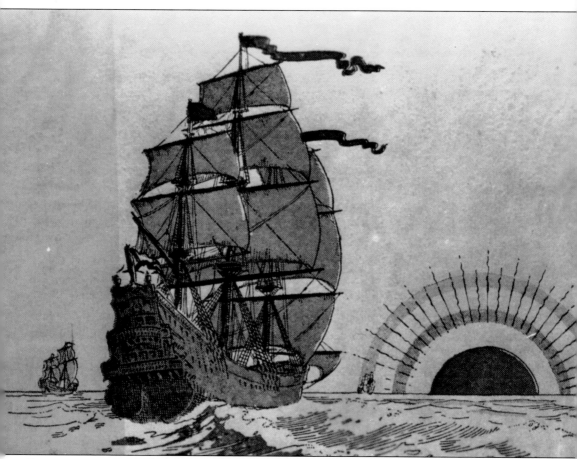

For over two centuries, the Manila-Acapulco galleons were the "spice line" for trade whose cargo included porcelain, processed silk cloth, and silver. With the trade came interaction among groups of people. Dances, diseases, food, language, and musical and visual arts were all a part of the exchange that took place at a more informal level. European Baroque music informed the music that followed. Elements of the mariachi's instrumentation, the practice of *Decima* in the Yucatan, and call and response from Africa are remnants of the trading and traveling that took place. Sailors and others were known to arrive at port and not return to ship. Music and art forms were shared, and new words were added to vocabularies; Asia and Europe became connected. The regular trips ended following Mexican Independence in 1822. (University of Southern California, USC Special Collections.)

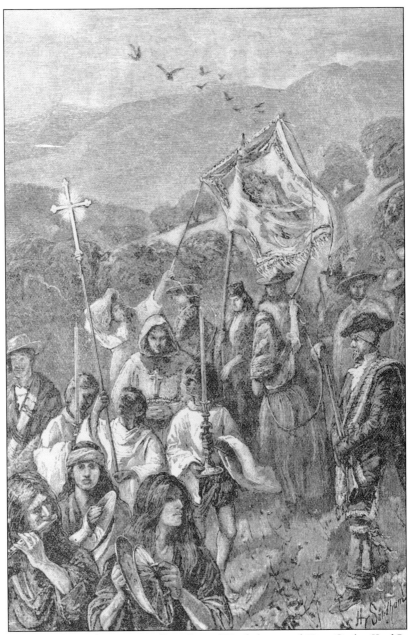

Establishment of colonies by Russians, French, and English caused King Carlos II of Spain great concern. Reinforcing and expanding settlements was seen as the solution: regents and soldiers would secure treasures, religion would secure souls. This image of the founders of Los Angeles in all likelihood bears a strong resemblance to those who settled in the San Gabriel Valley. Spanish culture of the 15th and 16th centuries reflected the influence of the Moors; Arabs and Africans had lived in Spain for five centuries. At one point, five different religious beliefs were a part of the Iberian Peninsula. The idea of *mestizaje*, or mixed heritage, was extremely common. Those who came to Nueva España were a group no less diverse than many communities of today. This image full of *mestizaje* looks like many who established the pueblos in Nueva España. (University of Southern California, USC Special Collections.)

Saving souls was to be the work of the mission system that was established in *Nueva España*. Fr. Junipero Serra led those who came to *Alta y Baja California*. He practiced mortification of the flesh in order to be more focused on the spiritual. His faith was committed and deep. There are those who felt he led his converts to salvation and those who felt he obliterated the sacred traditions of natives. Many he led shared kindness and love; others were brutal to the indigenous. Toypurina lived in the Misión San Gabriel and in response to treatment she saw, became a passionate advocate for her people. Her enemies called her sorceress; her allies viewed her as shaman. She was brought to trial, converted to Christianity, banished to Misión San Carlos, and married to soldier Manuel Montero. She died at age 39. (Both, University of Southern California, USC Special Collections.)

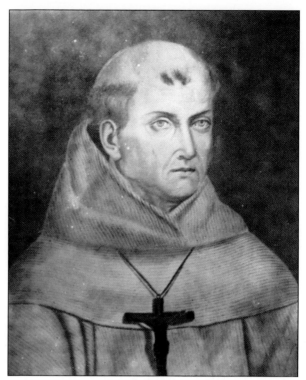

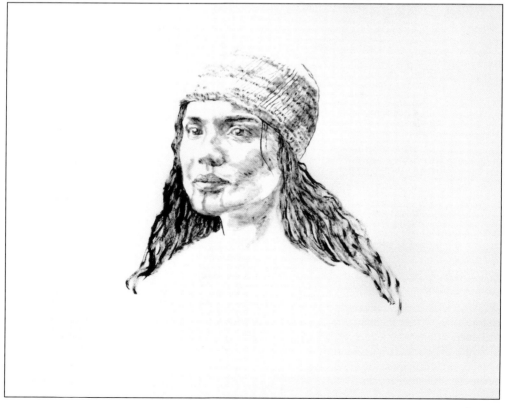

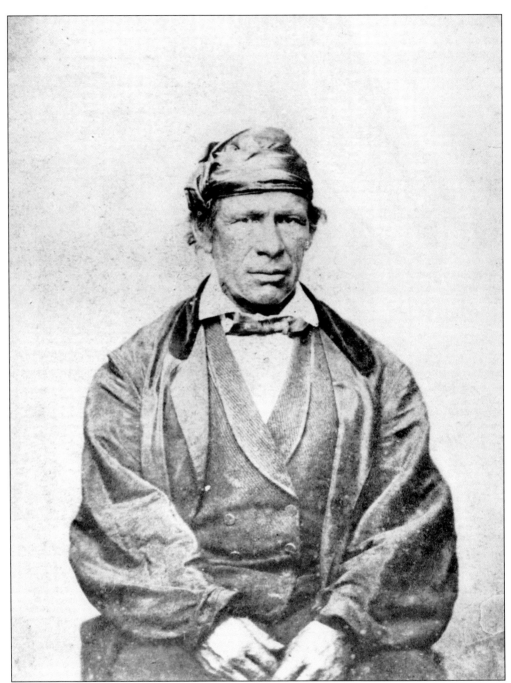

Marcos Alaniz is the son of a *Soldado de Cuera*. These soldiers who wore leather armor had the best training, as they had formalized practices and rules. Often from frontier areas themselves, they had a better understanding of terrain. *Teniente* (lieutenant), *Alferez* (ensign), *Cabos* (corporals), and *Sargentos* (sergeants) are words listed in documents of the time. Some soldados saw the military as a means of advancing in society. They were paid a salary or were on occasion given land grants. These men became parents to those who lived in *Baja y Alta California*. (University of Southern California, USC Special Collections.)

Two

HISPANO, MEXICANO, "CALIFORNIO," AMERICANO

The history of those living in *Alta y Baja California* was impacted by the history of the United States of Mexico and the history of the United States of America. In the span of 50 years, less than three generations, those living in Alta California were a part of four social systems and three different governments: Spanish, Mexican, and United States of America. The Mexican War of Independence from Spain (1810–1821) and the notion of Manifest Destiny produced two countries, one nascent and one developing, focused on retention versus expansion of land ownership as a core result of governmental policy. All of this altered the lives of those living at or connected with the missions. With independence from Spain came the secularization of land ownership. Land that had belonged to Spain and overseen by the Roman Catholic Church now became the property of individuals. On occasion, the recipients were indigenous or of moderate means. Many were soldiers, or their families, who had served crown and cross. All were distant from Spain; many had lived all of their lives in California. Some thought of themselves as Californios, a part of but separated from the *Estados Unidos de Mexico*. During their lives, Misión San Gabriel had become the richest in the mission system. It had supplied cattle, sheep, goats, hogs, horses, mules, and other supplies to settlements and missions throughout Alta California. Functioning as a plantation, it produced great wealth. At Misión San Gabriel, the Tongva Indian population grew from 1,201 in 1810 to 1,636 in 1820 and then declined to 1,320 in 1832. Nearly 6,000 Tongva lie buried in the grounds of the San Gabriel Mission. Many members of the Tongva were absorbed into Mexican society; with the secularization of land, records and identities were lost or not kept. The formalization of land ownership, by *Mexicano diseño* or American map, became increasingly more important. With the advent of U.S. laws, women lost the right of owning land in their names.

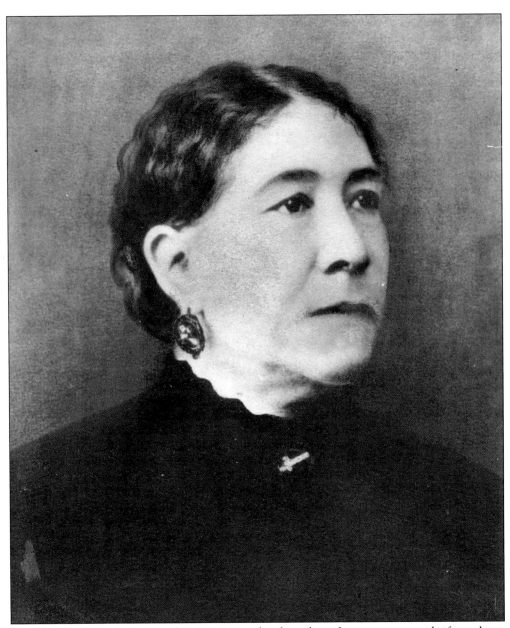

Doña Eulalia Perez de Guillen de Mariné is said to have been literate, was a midwife, and was devoted to church and family. She gave birth to 12 children; eight survived. In her oral history of 1877, Doña Eulalia shares that when she "came to San Diego from Loreto I was very fond of dancing and was considered the best dancer in the country." This image of her daughter Rita de la Ossa helps us imagine what Doña Eulalia may have looked like as a younger woman. Rita was one of five daughters who worked with Doña Eulalia at San Gabriel. In 1832, Vicente de la Ossa and Rita Guillen married. The next three decades of their lives reflected the ebb and flow of land ownership and the position of the native-born Californio in a changing society. Vicente knew those who shaped history, and he followed their lead. Rita, pregnant with their 13th child, survived him and ended her days in San Gabriel, where she had lived as a child. (Los Encinos State Historic Park Archives.)

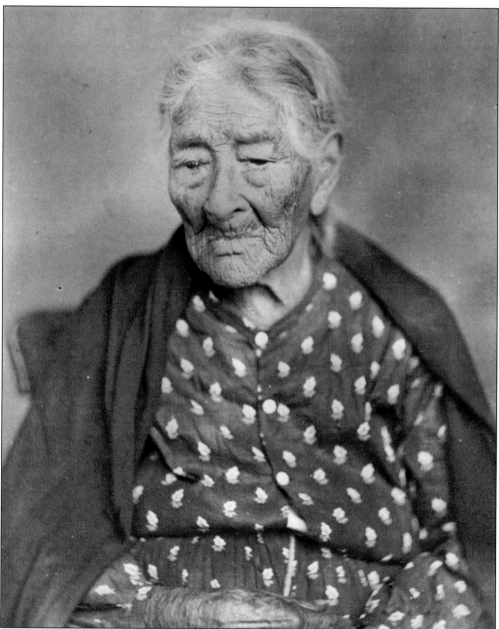

Eulalia Perez de Guillen de Mariné is one of the few interviewed for Bancroft Library who was not an aristocrat and one of even fewer who were women. Born in the military port of Loreto, Baja California, she traveled to Alta California as a soldier's wife and as a widow served as the *llavera* (keeper of keys) for Misión San Gabriel for 12 years. Capable, clever, and disciplined, she oversaw all that was not secular or military at the mission. When mission lands were secularized, the 14,000 acres of Rancho San Pascual—which later became Pasadena, San Marino, parts of La Cañada, Sierra Madre, and South Pasadena—were reserved for her. Charles Holder and Jeanne C. Carr wrote about her and her special place in Pasadena history. She is buried at her beloved mission. Exceptional even in death, she is one of the very few laypersons buried in an area reserved for the priests who served at Misión San Gabriel. (Bancroft Library, University of California, Berkeley.)

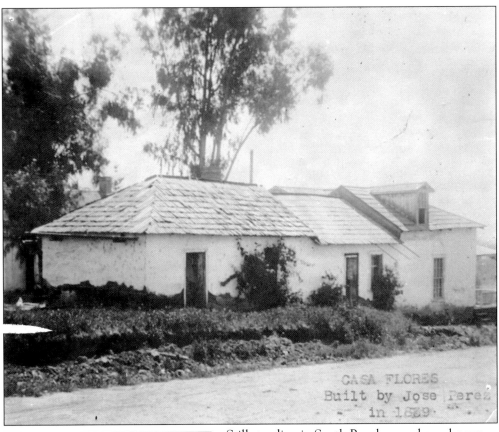

CASA FLORES
Built by Jose Perez
in 1829

Una Vieja
Sus Recuerdos

Dictados por Doña Eulalia Perez que
vivió en la Mision de San Gabriel a la Edad avanzada
de 139 años

a D. Tomas Savage
para la

Bancroft Library
1877

Still standing in South Pasadena and now known as the Flores Adobe, this was home to relatives of Juan Mariné. He was a soldier in late middle age when, at the encouragement of the mission fathers, he and Doña Eulalia married. Rancho San Pascual was formally deeded to Mariné on May 6, 1834. In her oral history, Doña Eulalia shares, "He only turned over half of the land to me and kept the other half." He died in 1838, leaving Doña Eulalia a widow for a second time. Through a series of transactions, Manuel Garfias eventually came to own Rancho San Pascual. Doña Eulalia had long left the land and had chosen to finish her last days at the homes of her daughters near her Misión San Gabriel. (Above, Pasadena Museum of History; at left, Bancroft Library, University of California, Berkeley.)

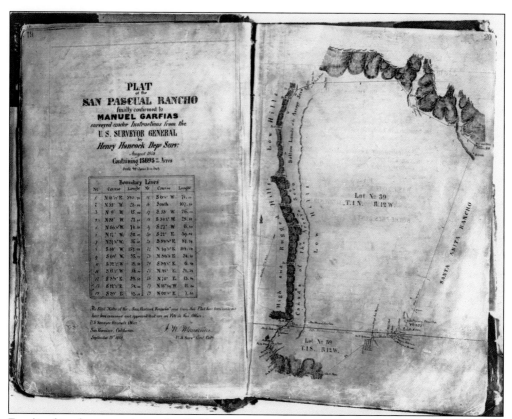

Few lived in the area prior to the Gold Rush of 1848. The vast majority of those living in the San Gabriel Valley, much as happens with any pioneering community, knew each other. Many, if not most, saw each other at the Misión San Gabriel, for at least the Holy Days. Because there were few settlers and more concern about ownership than disagreement about boundaries, a *diseño*, or map, could at times be open to interpretation. Owning land was seen as insurance for the future. Cattle were the immediate source of income. The brand on cattle often was generally more important than exact boundaries or vast amounts of land. (Both, Pasadena Museum of History.)

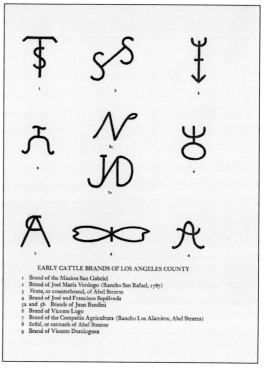

EARLY CATTLE BRANDS OF LOS ANGELES COUNTY

1 Brand of the Mission San Gabriel
2 Brand of José María Verdugo (Rancho San Rafael, 1787)
3 *Venta*, or counterbrand, of Abel Stearns
4 Brand of José and Francisco Sepúlveda
5a and 5b Brands of Juan Bandini
6 Brand of Vicente Lugo
7 Brand of the Compañía Agricultura (Rancho Los Alamitos; Abel Stearns)
8 *Señal*, or earmark of Abel Stearns
9 Brand of Vicente Domínguez

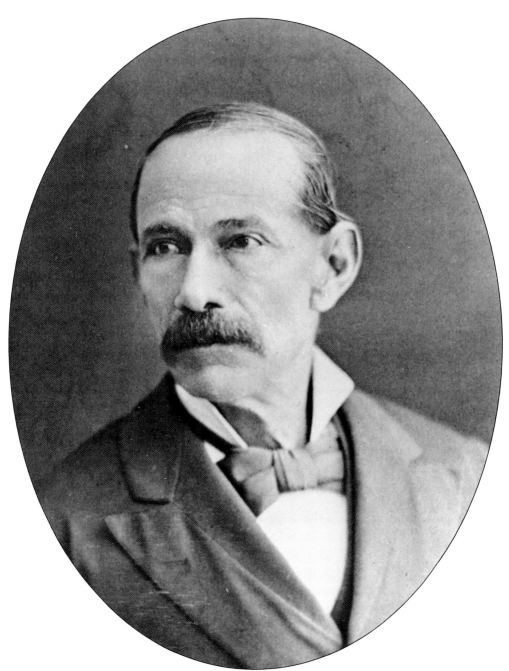

Many living in Alta California were connected via the *compadrazco* system, in which godparents were responsible for not only the religious upbringing of their godchild but were also often expected to help with fiscal support. This included keeping land within extended family and social units. Manuel Garfias received Rancho San Pascual from his mother-in-law, Doña Encarnacion Avila, who was granted the land by Gov. Manuel Micheltorena. Garfias served as a lieutenant under Micheltorena in the Mexican army during the Mexican-American War but became a part of the American government following the war. He served as pueblo councilman and as Los Angeles County treasurer from 1851 to 1853. (University of Southern California, USC Special Collections.)

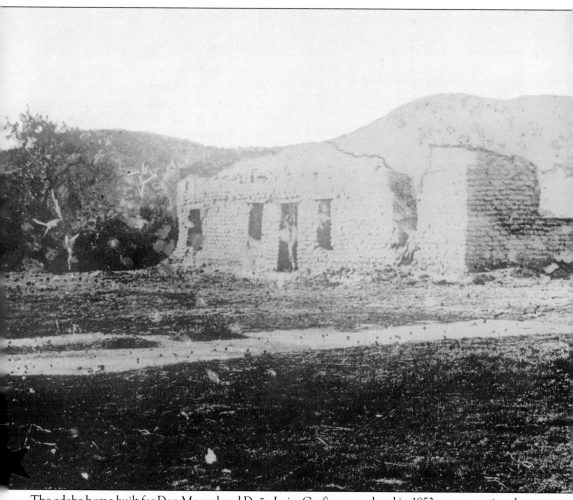

The adobe home built for Don Manuel and Doña Luisa Garfias, completed in 1853, was exceptional. Grand in size, two stories, and in modern quality, having green shutters, it was a novelty at the time. It is written that Garfias built a road to bring timber from a sycamore grove. His son, Manuel E. Garfias, was the first child of European heritage born on San Pascual soil. Many of the earliest English-speaking settlers knew about the adobe and spring but little of the man to whom it belonged. Articles later written about Garfias include mention of the adobe and of being the site where the first "white" baby is born. It was razed in the 1880s in the name of progress, according to Charles Adams, a 20th-century landscape architect and authority on adobes. (Pasadena Museum of History.)

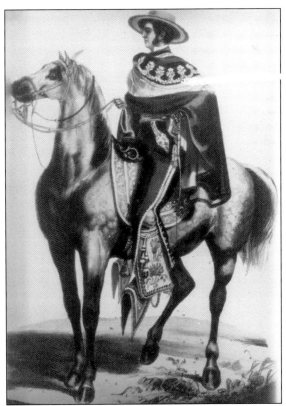

The "Californio" period is usually depicted as a romantic time of grace and comfort. For those who owned vast areas of land and could afford to be outfitted like this caballero, it was. It was also a time of clear hierarchy that lasted less than 30 years and was built upon the work of the Catholic Church and indigenous peoples. The neglected Tongva home beside the Misión San Gabriel reflects a different reality. Without the financial support they received during the viceregal era, from church and state, fields became fallow and a way of life gradually disappeared. (Both, University of Southern California, USC Special Collections.)

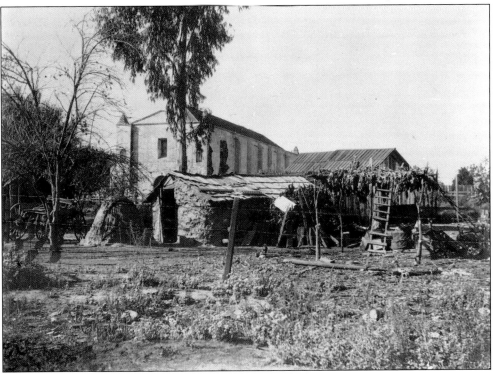

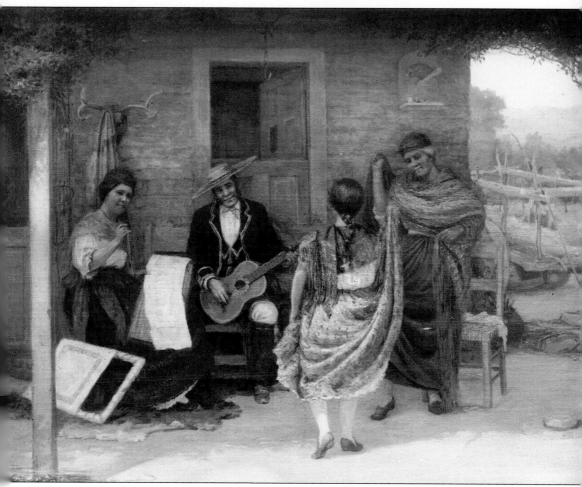

Living somewhat in isolation, older generations would share their reminiscences of songs, dances, and games that had been a part of their youth. For those living in Alta or Baja California, that would mean the music that had been *au courante* in their youth. Living far from cosmopolitan centers like Mexico City necessitated smaller, more intimate expressions of song and dance. It also supported ritual and tradition that kept what had been known, cherished, and practiced in a place far from the other established parts of *Nueva España*. (University of Southern California, USC Special Collections.)

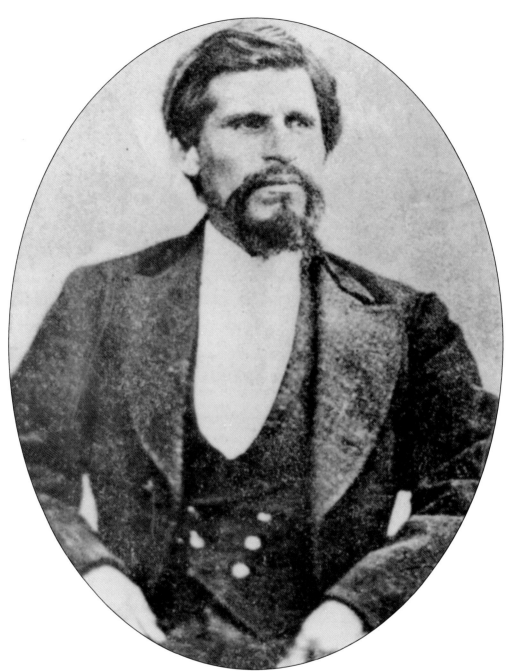

It is a known fact that Tiburcio Vasquez lived his last days as a wanted man. Why and how this came to be has long been discussed: some see him as a man who defied Colonial law and racial injustice and others see him as a *bandido*. Early residents of Pasadena like Hiram Reid, at some length in his *History of Pasadena*, describe him as being very polite. To quote him, "As Vasquez drew near he called out . . . and told them who he was; and one of his men who could speak English well introduced him assuring them that he was 'a perfect gentleman!' " A historical volume printed at the time of his death shares that students had the day off in order to view Vasquez in his cell the day before he was hanged. (University of Southern California, USC Special Collections.)

Three

RANCHOS TO RANCHES

In the state of California, cross-cultural interaction was taking place at many levels. Those from Durango or Zacatecas had traditions that were different from other *Mexicanos* from Veracruz or Baja California. The character and numbers of those who came to California for land, for gold, or for adventure also had a great impact. The miners who were from China, the United States and its territories, the countries of Latin American, or Europe found themselves in a new place with new customs and laws. There were also immigrants who left Europe or the East Coast and went to Mexico or its territories. The Western Hemisphere was a destination of opportunity. They learned the language of the land and followed its laws. In order to buy land, they became Mexican citizens and Roman Catholics, this being a legal requirement, at least on paper. Some immigrants embraced Mexican identity and culture. The antipathy and sympathy of those who had fought in the Mexican-American War as well as those who later fought the American Civil War influenced attitudes and social interaction in the area that became the city of Pasadena. Homesteaders who spoke Spanish all too often were referred to as squatters. Natural disasters like droughts and floods contributed to economic surges and recessions. The flux of the culture and of the time made it easier, and more likely, for intermarriages between groups to occur. Some marriages were made for love, some were made in order to secure family lands, and some were made looking to the future. Hubert Howe Bancroft, late-19th-century publisher, found Mexican and Californian history fascinating in its complexity. He found *memorias* and reports by officials a valuable source of information. Learning about Mexico was an interesting and profitable study. Several of the subjects of oral histories that were written for him and later published had lived in California when it was part of Mexico. Thomas Savage interviewed Miguel Blanco, Antonio Coronel, and Doña Eulalia Perez de Guillen de Mariné, each of whom was a part of Pasadena history.

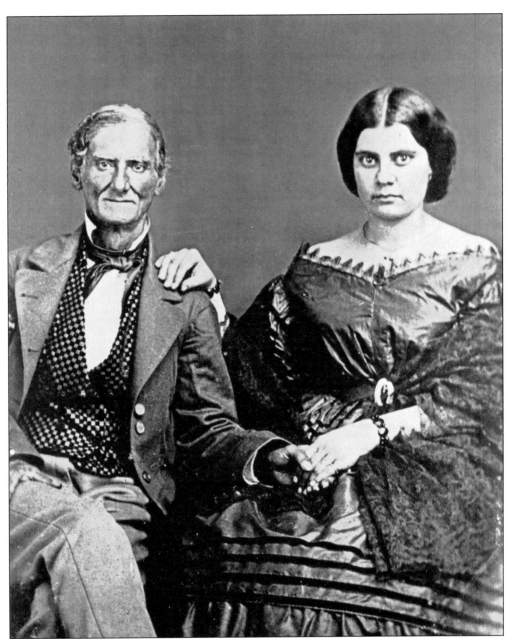

Don Juan Bandini was born in Peru, immigrated to Alta California, and eventually owned land from Tijuana to the San Bernardino Mountains. Richard Henry Dana describes him in some detail in *Two Years Before the Mast*. He is noted for being a dapper figure, fluent writer, and fine horseman. Trained as a lawyer, Don Juan served as administrator for Misión San Gabriel and was a business partner with Abel Stearns. His daughter-in-law, Helen Elliott Bandini, writes, "his . . . dances would cost as much as a thousand dollars . . . but as his income was at the time eighteen thousand a month it was not considered reckless expenditure." Initially supportive of the United States during the Mexican-American War, he became critical after the Land Act of 1851, which allowed Mexican land grants to be challenged. He is pictured here with his daughter Margarita. (Huntington Library.)

Don Abel Stearns, born in Massachusetts, the son of Levi and Elizabeth, went to Mexico and purchased land. By 1848, he owned several hundred thousand acres in Alta California. Astute in business affairs and lucky in love, he married the daughter of Juan Bandini, Arcadia. He and Hugo Reid were delegates to the First California Convention. In 1860, Stearns headed a household of 19, including his brother-in-law, 6-year-old Arturo Bandini. (Huntington Library.)

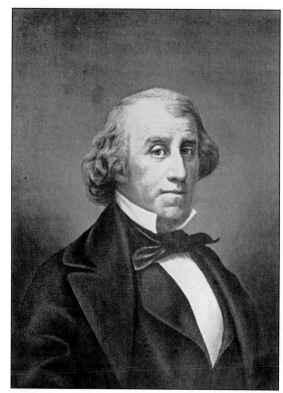

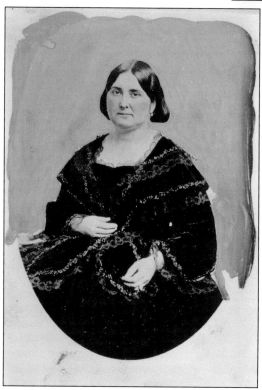

At 14, with a vast dowry in land, Arcadia Bandini married 43-year-old Stearns in 1839. After Stearns's death, she married Col. Robert L. Baker, owner of Rancho San Vicente y Santa Monica. Baker died in 1894. At her death in 1912, Arcadia was the wealthiest woman in California, leaving an estate of $7 to $8 million, no will, and no children in California. The estate was widely contested. (Autry National Center, Southwest Museum, Los Angeles; photograph P15380.)

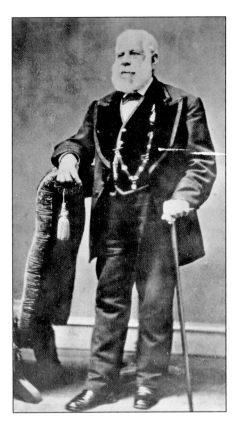

Don Pío Pico was born in the Misión San Gabriel; Doña Eulalia was midwife at his birth. His life was filled with great events; having been imprisoned for his political positions, he was the last Mexican governor of California and managed to survive the state's transition from the United States of Mexico to the United States of America. His parents, from Sonora, reflected the *meztizaje* of that area and era. (Huntington Library.)

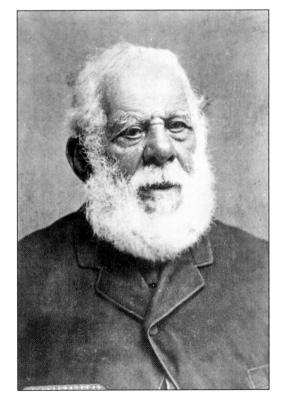

Former governor Pico's appearance seems to reflect his later life's experience. At the time of this portrait, he was 90 years old and impoverished. He had lost fortune, land, and, it seems, hope, thanks to poor business choices, gambling debts, and loss of property to loan usurers. Having lost his deed to his *ranchito*, he died in poverty at his daughter's house in Los Angeles at the age of 91. (Huntington Library.)

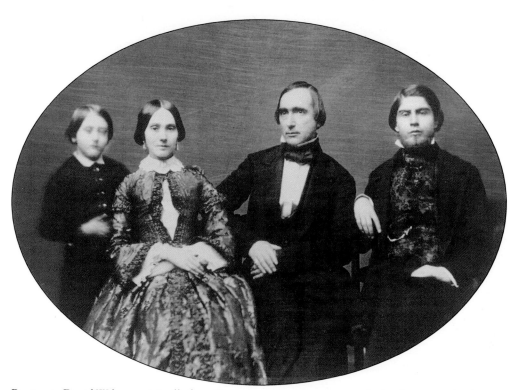

Benjamin David Wilson, originally from Tennessee, became a noteworthy landowner and politician in the San Gabriel Valley in the area that was to become Pasadena. His first wife, Ramona, was of the wealthy Yorba family. Don Benito Wilson was the first non-native mayor of Los Angeles, served in the California senate, and bought Rancho San Pascual from Manuel Garfias. He is pictured here with his second wife, Margaret Hereford, and their family. (Huntington Library.)

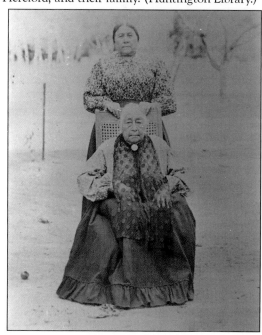

Englishman Michael White was known as Miguel Blanco following his marriage to María del Rosario Guillen. In 1877, he was interviewed for Howard Bancroft at his home, now part of San Marino. His oral history "All the Way Back to 1828" relates his view of the interaction of Americans, Mexicans, and American Indians. Pictured here are his relatives Maria de Los Angeles Guillen (seated) and Maria de Jesus Lopez. (San Marino Historical Society.)

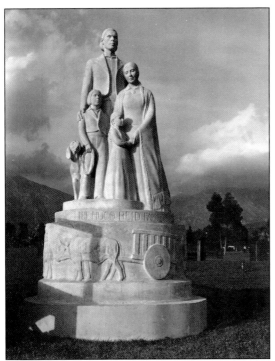

Hugo Reid, born in Scotland, traveled to Peru and became a partner in a mercantile business. While in Los Angeles, he met and began a new partnership with Abel Stearns. He also met and fell in love with Bartolomea Comicrabit. After her husband's death, they married, becoming "Don Perfecto" and Victoria Reid. In 1852, he wrote letters to the *Los Angeles Star* regarding the culture, history, and religion of the Tongva. (Security Pacific Collection/ Los Angeles Public Library.)

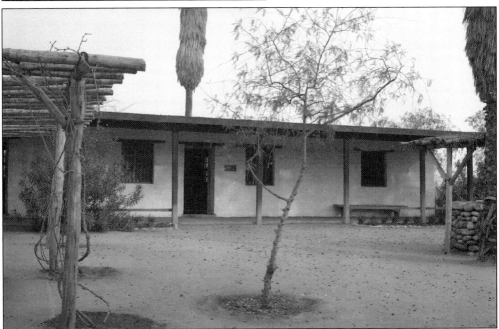

As an infant, Bartolomea was baptized at the Misión San Gabriel. She married early, and with her husband, Pablo Maria, had four children. She may have been taught to read by Doña Eulalia and lived her life within the social structure of *Nueva España*. She was given a land grant—Rancho Huerta de Cuati—which she later sold to Benjamin D. Wilson. Victoria finished her life at the Misión San Gabriel. Pictured here is the restored adobe of Victoria and Don Perfecto. (Pasadena Museum of History.)

Don Antonio F. Coronel joined
the Mexican army during the war
between the United States and
Mexico. Following the signing of
the Treaty of Guadalupe Hidalgo, he
became a citizen of the United States,
serving as state treasurer from 1866
to 1870. He was a charter member of
the Historical Society of Southern
California and is pictured here with
his wife, Doña Mariana. His image
graced the 1904 Tournament of Roses
program. (Huntington Library.)

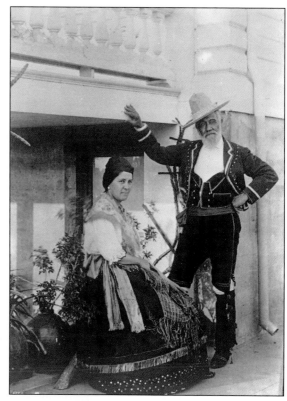

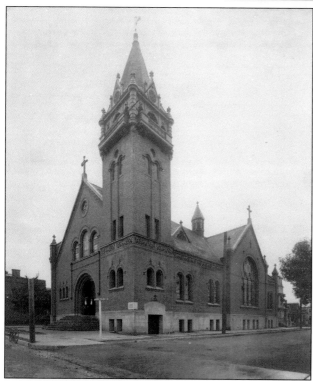

In 1886, Fr. Patrick Harnett of
Los Angeles was assigned to
create a parish in the Pasadena
area. This is an image of the
second building that served St.
Andrew's parish at the corner of
Fair Oaks Avenue and Walnut
Street. The establishment of
the parish began a separation of
Catholic Latinos from the San
Gabriel Mission. Parishioners
became distanced from their
historical and religious roots.
(Pasadena Museum of History.)

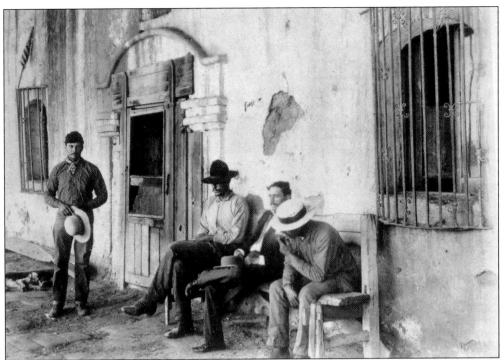

Born of a family of great wealth, as it was measured in the "Californio" era, Arturo Bandini benefitted from the financial and social position of his parents and grandparents. He was educated at St. Vincent's Academy and Santa Clara College, earning his bachelor of arts and his master of arts. In the 1880s, he was a sheep rancher, wool being a vital material. He appears in this picture taken at Mision San Fernando Rey de España, head covered by a dark hat, mostly obscuring his face. He is standing, hat in hand, in the picture below. (Above, Autry National Center, Southwest Museum, Los Angeles, photograph P18893; below, Pasadena Museum of History.)

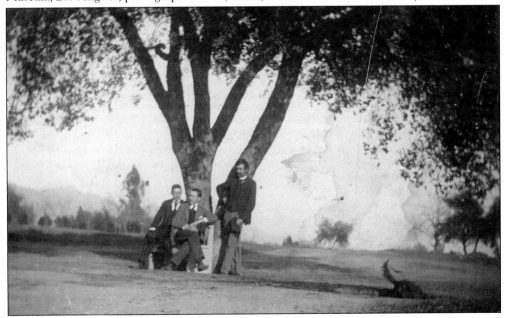

Four

BECOMING PASADENA

The earliest English-speaking settlers to come to Rancho San Pascual were apparently comfortable with, if not fluent in, speaking some Spanish. The Tongva were called the San Pascual Indians. The Arroyo Seco retained its name, other area names were altered; Las Flores Canyon lost its adjective order and retained its article, Rubio Canyon, and Prieto Canyon became Anglicized. Rancho San Pascual, following the Mexican-American War, was designated Rancho San Pasqual. It is possible the misspelling is a simple clerical mistake; it is also possible the revised name resonated with Americans who successfully won the Battle of San Pasqual not far from San Gabriel. Writers of the era used words like *zanjero* or *vaquero* with the same ease as referring to them as orchardist or businessman. English-speaking Robert Owen, the wealthiest black man in the state, sent his *vaqueros* to help free Biddy Mason. Owners of large landholdings began to develop or sell the land for financial profit. Grapevines and orchards became a means of commerce, and workers were needed. Peoples of many languages and from many nations worked in orchards and on railroads. The place names of the Tongva had become names like Indian Flats. As this transpired in California, Daniel Berry suffered from asthma in Indiana. Some of his neighbors and his relatives were tired of the cold and were ready to move west. Much was written of the California Colony of Indiana established in 1874; what is not often noted is that Berry stayed at the Pico House in Los Angeles while he looked for land, water, and the developing means of transportation in the San Gabriel Valley. By the time the city of Pasadena was established in 1886, this agrarian region was becoming industrialized, albeit with simple mechanical technology. The migration of labor barons, the social elite, and the Depression of 1893 led to a new social structure. What was written on paper or shared in conversation became fact to those who were to move to Pasadena and call it home. By 1910, speaking Spanish, especially as one's dominant language, was not seen as beneficial or as a virtue.

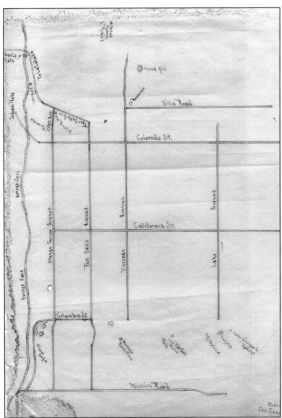

Albert Lee Carr's parents, Ezra and Jeanne, were influential in the life of John Muir and of early Pasadena. Jeanne Carr writes of the need to "preserve the interesting story of her (Doña Eulalia's) life." This map shares something of the same sensibilities. Major streets and natural elements are noted, as are the names of the property of *Mexicanos* no longer in the area; names are grammatically correct in both languages. (Carr Collection, Pasadena Museum of History.)

The image is somewhat unclear, but the symbolism may be all too clear. Don Pio Pico having become something of an anachronism—a part of California's mythic past—drew people like Jeanne Carr to see him or other "Californios" and have their picture taken of or with them. This image seems to reflect changes in the area from Rancho San Pascual to San Pasqual Ranch to Pasadena, California. (Security Pacific Collection/Los Angeles Public Library.)

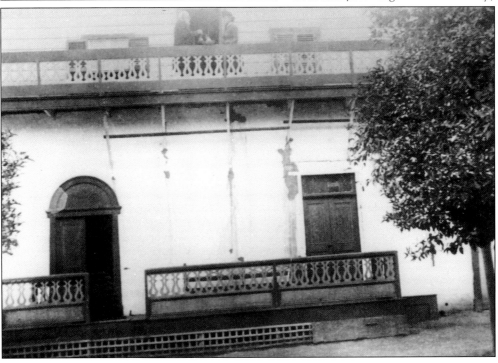

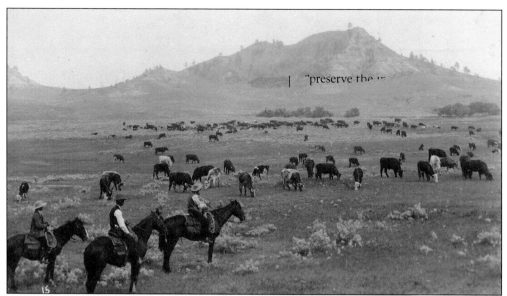

"preserve the ·

The cause of death of Antonio Velazquez is a mystery. An 1898 article shares the names of the boys who found his body by a strychnine bottle. Velazquez's daughter and son are not named, but the daughter is quoted as saying that she "could not reason for his taking his own life, except that he was too old to work." It is further reported that he was an old Spaniard and was a well-known character, having lived in Pasadena over 40 years. Perhaps he simply could work no more or didn't have the skills that were useful in a Pasadena that was quickly becoming a part of the 20th century. Pictured here are men who worked in the area, who also had to deal with changing times and the decreasing needs for their talents. (Above, Pasadena Museum of History; below, Security Pacific Collection/Los Angeles Public Library.)

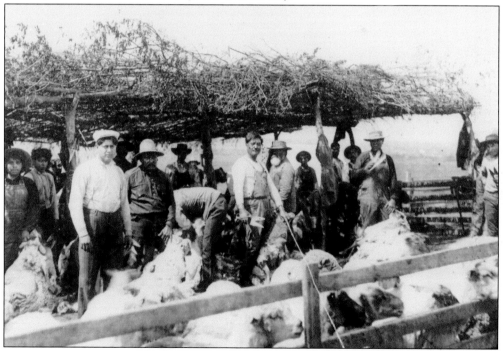

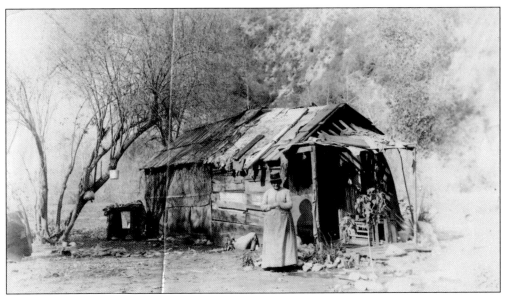

Indiana Colony members, homesteaders, and squatters lived in the area at the same time. There is spotty information about the homesteaders and squatters. The reverse of this photograph reads, "Mex/Am dwelling in the Arroyo 1897." Carlos R. Cruz, born in California in 1832, applied for a homestead and later sold his property for $2,000. The trees he planted still stand in Eaton Canyon, but there is no known image of him. (Pasadena Museum of History.)

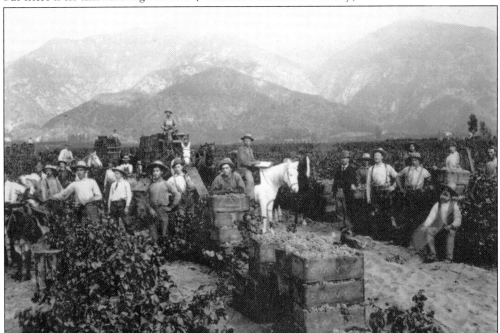

Charles Cook Hastings purchased land in 1882. On his Mesa Alta Rancho, now known as Hastings Ranch, he planted grapevines and constructed a mansion. The vastness of his ranch, like others in the San Gabriel Valley, needed large numbers of workers, many of whom were immigrants from Mexico. They often worked in the fields with blacks, Chinese, Greeks, Irish, and Japanese as land ownership had become almost exclusively Euro-American. (Pasadena Museum of History.)

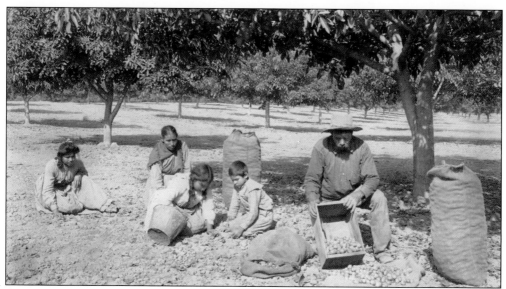

A new immigrant wave came at the dawn of the 20th century to Pasadena and the San Gabriel Valley. Some came as a result of one of the three droughts that affected areas of Northern Mexico and the Southwest United States. Some had left played-out mines of the northern states of Mexico or the U.S. territories of Arizona and New Mexico. Others had been brought to work on railways by industrialists' agents or left poverty that had grown during the incumbency of Mexican president Porfirio Diaz. Some worked on the 300-acre sewer farm owned by the City of Pasadena. Then as now, it was common for immigrant families to work as a unit. The sewer farm quit selling walnuts in 1914 because of public concerns regarding farm practices. (Above, Pasadena Museum of History; below, Pasadena Museum of History.)

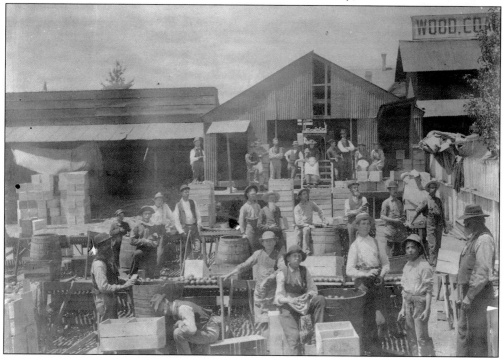

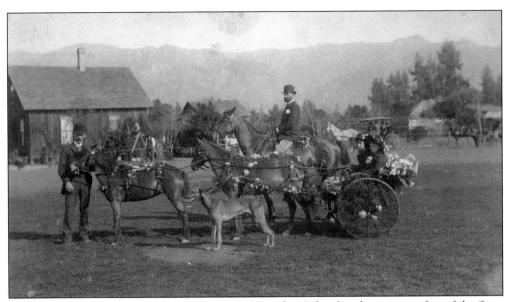

Arturo Bandini spoke five languages, organized Pasadena's first band, was a member of the Sons of the Golden West, and was an organizer and patron of the Tournament of Roses; he and James de Barth Shorb, son-in-law of B. D. and Ramona Wilson, were honorary members of the Valley Hunt Club. Between 1893 and 1897, he served as Los Angeles County deputy county clerk, assessor, tax collector, and auditor. He was executor to Arcadia de Baker's fortune. Pictured is an entry from the first parade. (Pasadena Museum of History.)

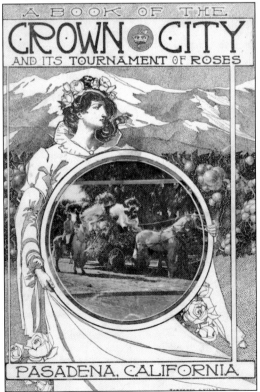

The Tournament of Roses has been a part of Pasadena since 1890 thanks to members of the Valley Hunt Club. Early post-parade events included "traditional Early Spanish" games and skills—usually led by Arturo Bandini or members of his family. The cover text of the 1907 Tournament of Roses program has Spanish phrases woven in the text and cover graphics by Los Angeles native Hernando G. Villa. (Pasadena Museum of History.)

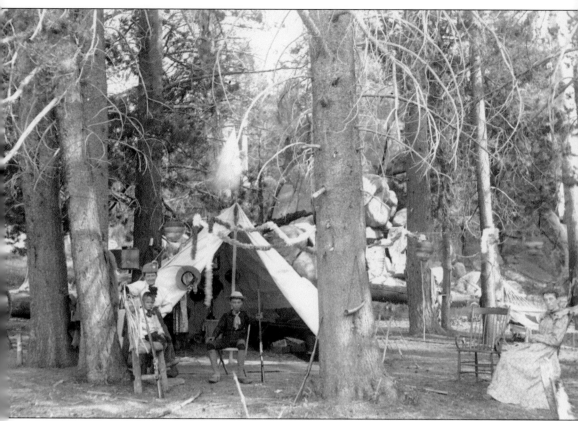

Helen "Nelly" Elliott was an independent spirit. She moved to California with her parents and siblings; was a founder of the Presbyterian church in Pasadena; married the family's boarder, Arturo Bandini; wrote a history of California that was used as a state textbook; and was a friend of both T. P. Lukens and Charles Lummis. She was involved with women's suffrage and Native American affairs and was among the founders of the Shakespeare Club. She often wrote about the culture of 19th-century California. In this photograph taken by T. P. Lukens are, from left to right, Nelly, her children Ralph and Elliott Bandini, and her mother, Helen Elliott, of the Indiana Colony. Other photographs show Nelly in a variety of garb, including an outfit that reflects the Spanish-American culture she often wrote about. As an adult, her son Ralph, along with other members of the Hispanic Society of California, donated the building of the Casa de Adobe, adjacent to the Southwest Museum. It was modeled after Rancho Guajome, home to his relatives Ysidora Bandini and Cave Johnson Couts. (Pasadena Museum of History.)

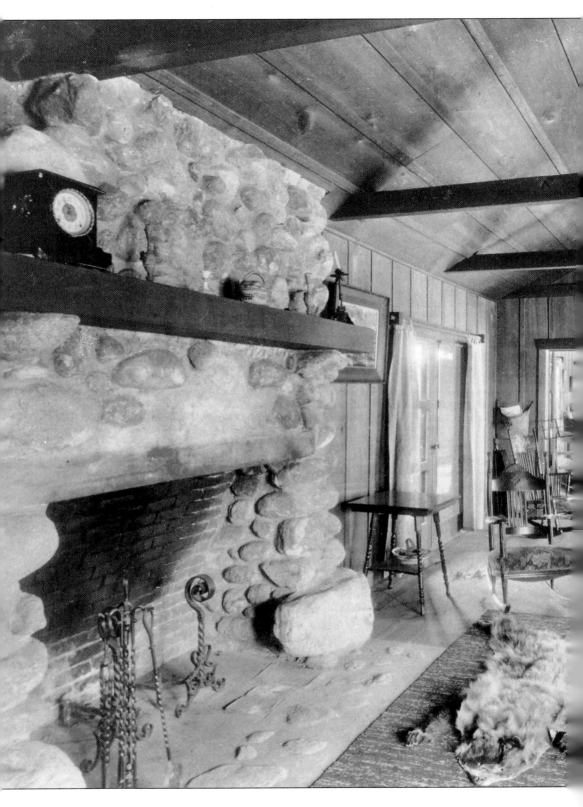

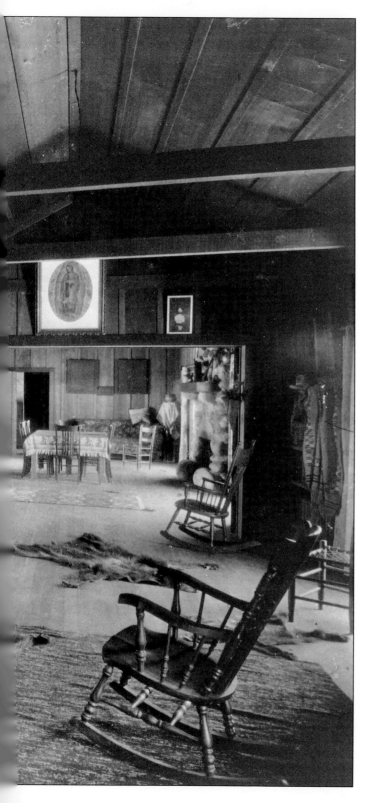

In 1903, Arturo and Helen Elliott Bandini approached brother architects Charles and Henry Greene. They wanted a home that would reflect their love of the out-of-doors and be reminiscent of the ranchos of 19th-century California. The finished home reflected elements of the rancho style, incorporating exposed rafters and interaction between outdoor and indoor spaces. The landscaping was sparse; words like sustainable or xeriscaped were used to describe plant design. The view of the great room has simple furniture, a well-used hearth, and a bearskin rug and is replete with an image of the Virgen de Guadalupe over a lintel. Although there was much community concern and discussion, it was demolished in the 1960s. Its demolition sadly predated the preservation movement that grew in Pasadena in the late 20th century. (Avery Library, Columbia University.)

41

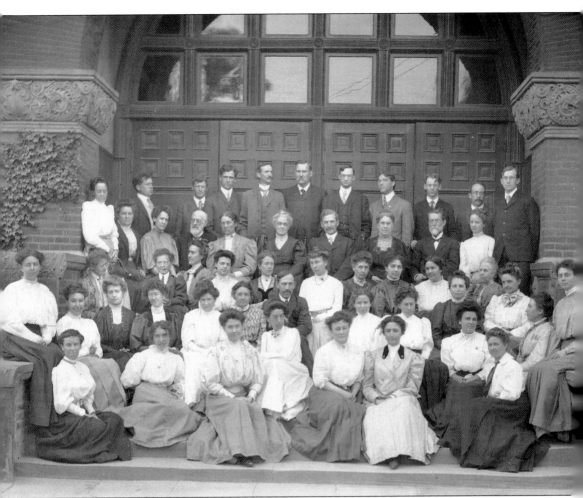

Maria de Guadalupe Evangelina Lopez was raised at the San Gabriel Mission and received her early education in Pasadena. She graduated from Pasadena High School in 1897 with a scientific major, performed the *Capriccioso*, op.14 by Mendelssohn at the graduation exercise, which took place in Pasadena at the Grand Opera House, went to the Normal School (teaching college), and was noted in the *Pasadena Star* as being the youngest professor at the University of Southern California in 1902. By the time she was a part of this group picture, she was married to Hugh Lowther, who became a teacher at Occidental College. She worked at UCLA as a translator and when she retired volunteered in San Gabriel, living in her ancestral adobe called ala Casa Vieja or Adobe Lopez de Lowther. She was known variously as Lupe, Eva, Maria, and Marie. She is listed as being in the picture, but it is unclear where she is seated. (University of Southern California, USC Special Collections.)

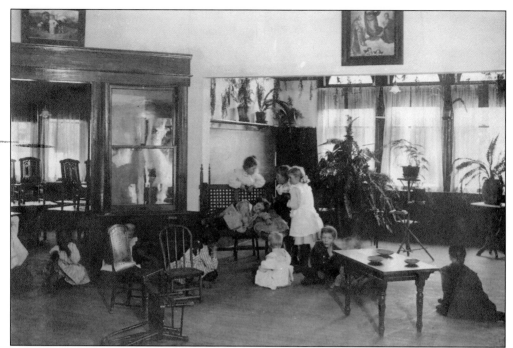

The San Pascual District was established in 1874. In 1878, a Central School was built on land donated by Benjamin Wilson. Over the next century, schools would be moved, renamed, or built depending upon educational and social philosophies, as well as numbers of students. In a 1937 partial archiving of school-related materials, the following is found: "Garfield School; second grade 1902. First dramatization class in the public school." (Pasadena Unified School District.)

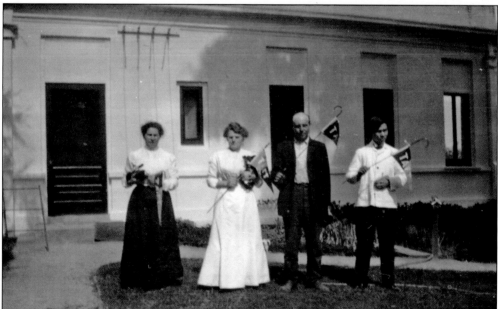

Orange Grove, commonly called Millionaires Row, had homes that required staff. This photograph is from a scrapbook of Eva Scott Fenyes who lived on Orange Grove. The staff holding banners saluting visiting president William Taft are, from left to right, Mina, Catherine, William, and Joe.

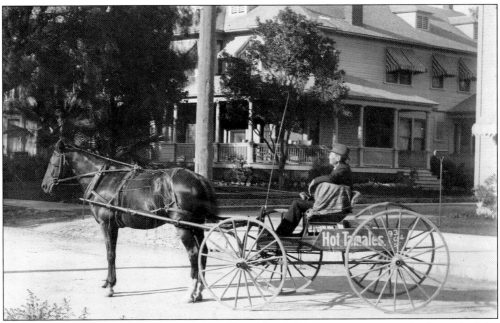

Street food vendors have long been a part of Pasadena's business community. At the end of the 19th century, vendors could be heard with pitches like "Ice for sale" and "Get your red hot dogs." The tamale vendor pictured above was a member of this enterprising group. Abalenio Hernandez is listed in the 1910 census as living at 615 South Broadway with his wife, Rita. He is 50 years old and is listed as having immigrated to the United States in 1895. One has to wonder if Rita was the silent partner who made the tamales. One can also wonder which of the children in this undated Pasadena School District picture might have tasted his wares. (Both, Pasadena Museum of History.)

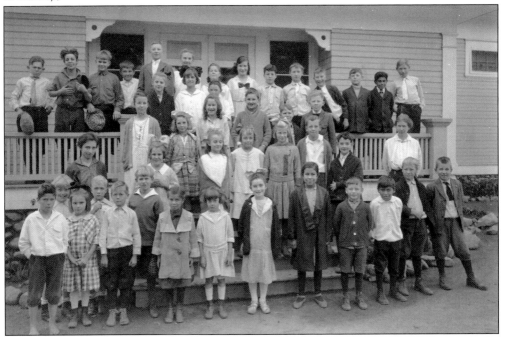

Five

DEFINING IDENTITY

The experiences of members of the *Mexicano* and Mexican American community became ever more varied as the 20th century progressed. Wynona/Cypress, or Northside, became a neighborhood where African American, Japanese American, and Mexican American families lived next door to each other. Sonora became known as the Southside and was a barrio, *gente* (people) living together who had a common language, many working initially at jobs related to the Pacific Electric Railway. "Roger" Mejia shares that if lost one could ask someone for help. A third area to the east of Pasadena was called Chihuahuita, or Titleyville, depending on one's dominant language. Because of its distance from the city, Chihuahuita had a school, two stores, and two churches. The stores were established by Beatriz Torres, a Mexican who was Catholic, and by Harry Aron, a Russian who was Jewish, both living in Chihuahuita. The Roman Catholic and Methodist churches were on the same block. Gradually the youth, and some adults, felt closer to the United States of America than to the Estados Unidos de México. There were those who benefitted from living for sometime in the area, receiving an education, and then going on to college or professions. Like other groups portrayed in literature, movies, and often theater, at the time, there was a fine line between symbol, stereotype, and caricature. The *Mission Play* and the *Ramona Pageant* reinforced these perceptions; the line between reality and roles became blurred. The experience of the Californio became mythology, and the laborer of the fields or the railways often became viewed as a foreigner, sometimes in the land of their birth. Progressives, social workers, and teachers were dedicated to helping the Mexican families become better assimilated and acculturated in the American way, while not losing some of their traditions. Social worker Frances Boniface lived in Chihuahuita and worked at the Mexican Settlement. Nellie Russ, librarian for the Pasadena Public Library, purchased documents on the early history of California, which included manuscripts in Spanish.

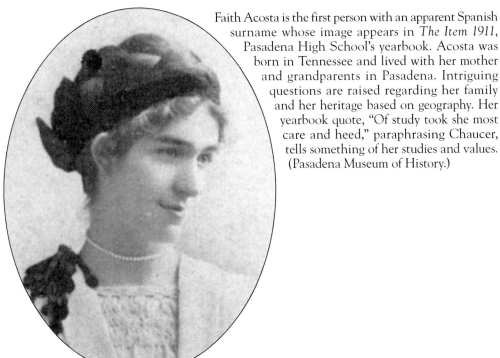

Faith Acosta is the first person with an apparent Spanish surname whose image appears in *The Item 1911*, Pasadena High School's yearbook. Acosta was born in Tennessee and lived with her mother and grandparents in Pasadena. Intriguing questions are raised regarding her family and her heritage based on geography. Her yearbook quote, "Of study took she most care and heed," paraphrasing Chaucer, tells something of her studies and values. (Pasadena Museum of History.)

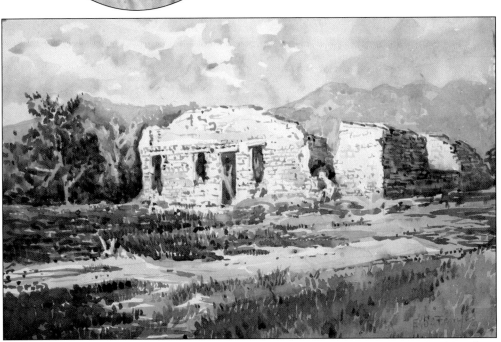

Eva Scott Fenyes loved to travel and was a patron of the arts and a painter of considerable talent. Her interest in and appreciation of Californiana expressed itself in small ways like this watercolor and in much larger places like support of the Southwest Museum. The image here, painted in 1916, is of the Garfias Adobe, probably based on an 1884 photograph. (Autry National Center, Southwest Museum, Los Angeles, photograph FEN.139.)

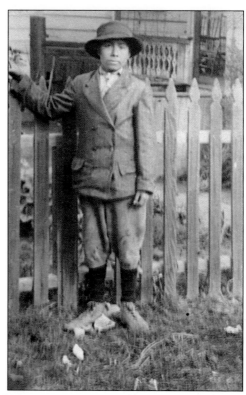

During the middle of 19th century, the well-positioned, by station or wealth, could afford to be photographed. Photographs were also taken as a way of memorializing commercial ventures, events, and groups. In the early 20th century, the person of average means began to have his or her picture taken. The faces of the adults in the earliest studio images often express a combination of concern, curiosity, and formality. This was also true for Mexican American children in Pasadena. Joe Meza (right), in Chihuahuita in his lovingly altered suit and well-worn shoes, seems at the age where the import of the photograph matters to him. Stella Nuñez, in the Wynona/Cypress area, seems more concerned with the bird in the hand and the person who placed her on the chair. (At right, Pasadena Museum of History; below, Daniel and Stella Castro Collection.)

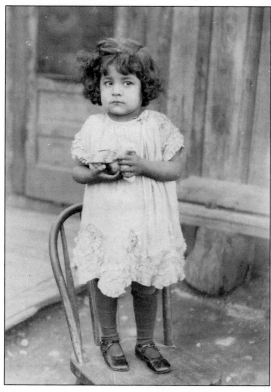

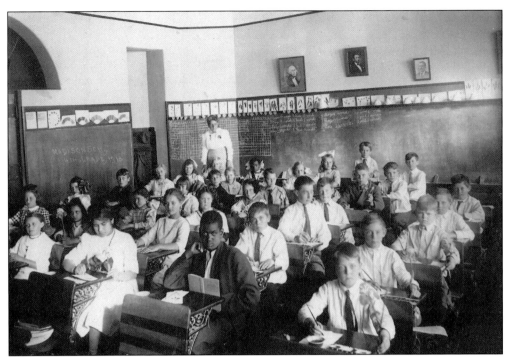

The clarity of the 1913 image of Madison School's fourth grade is stunning. Among the striking aspects is the degree of integration in the classroom and of the curriculum. The students are posed, dressed in their apparent best, while participating in what appears to be an art/botany activity. While it is easy to note those of African American heritage, it is more challenging to identify which students may be of Latino heritage. Most of the children in this very formal pose seem aware of the camera and their expected behavior. By contrast, the 1914 group of students at Garfield Elementary appear of a shared heritage. The spectrum of wear of their clothes runs from crisp white to clean and worn, and shoes range from new to lacking a sole to nonexistent. The picture is taken outside on the school steps, allowing for a special moment between kindred spirits. (Above, Pasadena Museum of History; below, Pasadena Museum of History.)

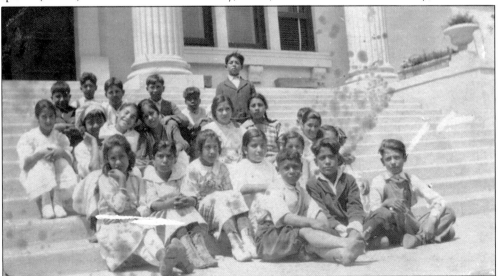

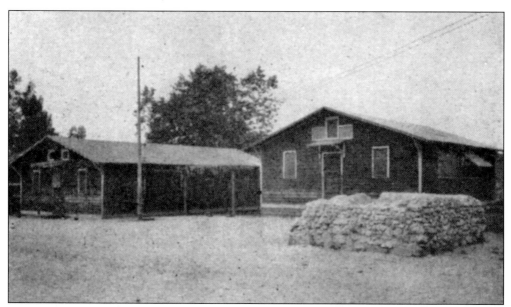

It was not uncommon to have segregated schools for Mexicans in the West, as there were segregated schools for blacks in the South. Established in 1915 as Titleyville School, the name was changed the next year to Chihuahuita; its student body was almost exclusively *Mexicano* and Mexican American. It was renamed John C. Fremont School in 1923 and continued to serve a similar student population through the 1950s. (Pasadena Unified School District.)

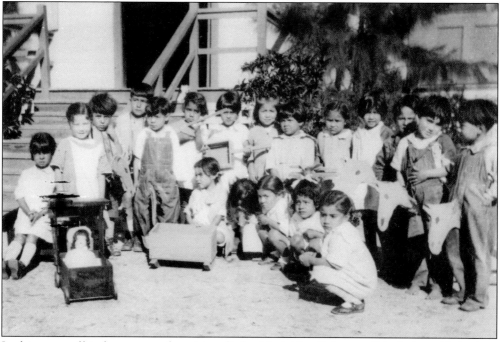

In this group of kindergartners, there is one little girl who has light eyes, light hair, and light skin. She may be a *Mexicana*, one of her parents may be of European ancestry, or she may be the child of German, Jewish, Russian, or British extraction who lived in the area. In any case, she is one of the children posing with toys in front of the school. (Segura Collection.)

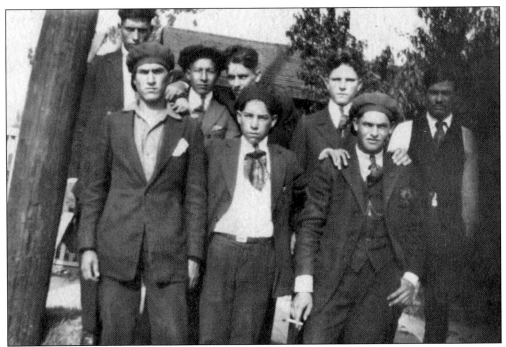

These young men on Fair Oaks in 1917 are sending a message; how much it may be real and how much may be posturing was probably known at the time. The names written on the picture's back include Heliberto, Simon, Joe Meza, Manual Lara, Tony C., Trini O., Joe L., and an illegible name. This part of Pasadena was referred to as the Sonora or Southern section. (Pasadena Museum of History.)

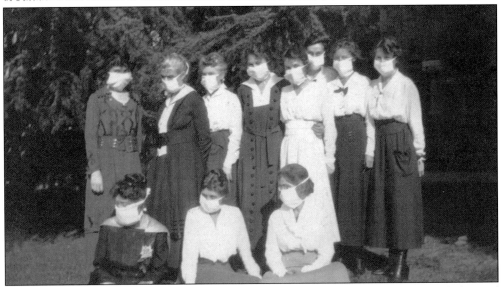

These Pasadena librarians wearing masks reflect their commitment to sharing knowledge and to the gravity of the influenza pandemic of 1918, commonly referred to as the Spanish Flu. At the time, children were kept out of school in some places for months at a time. Goya Misquez, as an octogenarian, shared her childhood memories of learning to count by seeing the number of people who went into a clinic and counting the number of those later carried out. (Pasadena Public Library.)

It was common for *Mexicanos* and Mexican Americans to marry at a young age. Because of isolation and segregation, young men and women had gone to school and church together and socialized with each other for most of their lives; marriage seemed the next step after high school. In this wedding photograph, José Meza wears a suit that is modern in cut, and Petra wears a more traditional bridal gown. It was at this time that Christine Lofstedt wrote her thesis, "A Study of the Mexican Population in Pasadena, California." The first page includes the following information: total Mexican population of 1,736. Of that, 20 percent or 350 persons live in Chihuahuita; 25 percent or 402 persons live in the Northern section; and 57 percent or 984 persons live in the Southern section. Studies like this were used to support work done with the Mexican community, including the Settlement House and Broadway Courts. (At right, Meza Collection, Pasadena Museum of History; below, Pasadena Museum of History.)

A STUDY OF THE MEXICAN POPULATION
IN PASADENA, CALIFORNIA.

Pasadena, California has a foreign population of Mexicans that is large enough to call for consideration, and small enough to be handled intelligently and effectively.

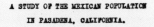

TABLE I.

PEOPLE

PERSONS IN EACH SECTION.

	Number.	Percent.
Chihuahuita	350	20
Northern Section	402	25
Southern Section	984	57
TOTAL	1,736	100

In June, 1922, Pasadena had within its gates a total Mexican population of 1,736. This population can be divided into three groups. The Southern Section is located in that narrow strip of land south of Colorado Street, traversed by two railroad tracks, having gas tanks, electric power plants, several factories, laundries, and a heterogeneous huddle of abodes. This small Industrial section is

Pasadena Mexican Survey, 1922.

NOTE:- The above Survey was made February 13 to June 1st., 1922, under the auspices of the Pasadena Chamber of Commerce. Miss Edith Howard,B.S.,Stanford University,conducted the Survey. Having been a teacher in Mexican Settlements, speaking the language, and having the happy faculty of gaining the confidence of the Mexicans,the result of Miss Howard's investigation is unquestionably as authentic as any that can be secured among these people.

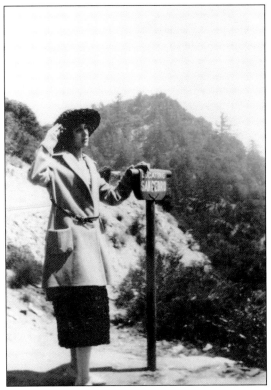

In the 1920s, the experiences within the Latino community reflected several waves of immigration. Some were recent arrivals because of the Mexican Revolution, which ebbed and flowed from 1910 to 1920. Others may have arrived as a response to the Cristero War, where the anti-Catholic government and Catholic population fought each other. Yet others were members of families that had been living in the United States long enough to have some discretionary income. It is possible that the young woman at Mount Lowe at left may be a day visitor from Los Angeles. She may have ridden through the main streets in Pasadena and not realized that there were *Mexicano* and Mexican American communities here. Frank and Jess, seated on the pole, show a timeless energy shared between big and little brothers. (At left, Security Pacific Collection/Los Angeles Public Library; below, Pasadena Museum of History.)

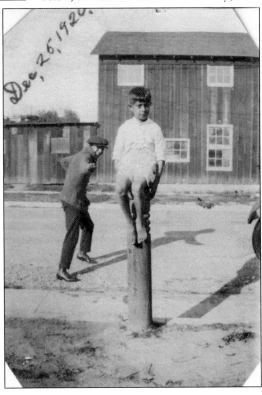

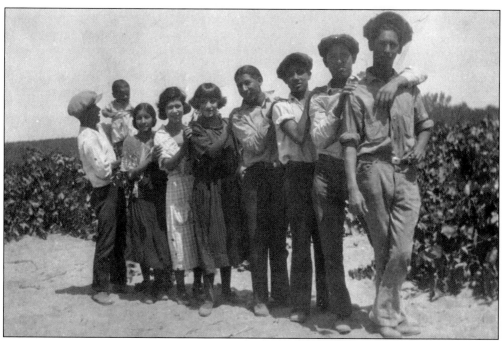

Someone in the Meza family loved to take pictures and could afford to do so. It seems there was a good bit of humor shared regularly and a sense of the theatrical. The photograph in Sierra Madre (above) at the Arroyo mud hole (below) includes members of the older generation in addition to the young people striking modern poses. According to headlines in the *Pasadena News*, from 1914 until 1919 the city set aside "Wednesday for Negroes, Mexicans and Orientals: Commission chooses Thursday for women" as days when Brookside Plunge was open to them. Enjoying the plunge on the weekend as a family would not have been possible until 1947, when the plunge was desegregated under the leadership of Dr. Edna Griffin. (Above, Archives at the Pasadena Museum of History; below, Archives at the Pasadena Museum of History.)

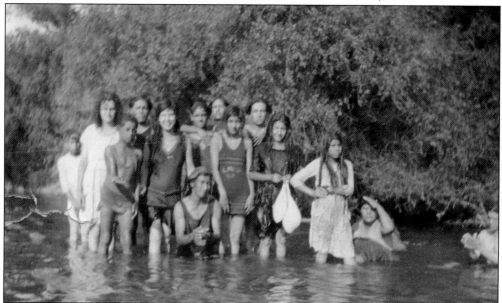

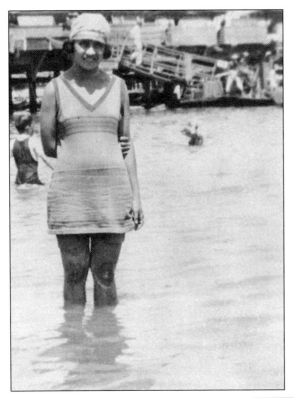

Within the span of a generation, some young people began to identify with the images they saw in American advertisements, magazines, and movies. With the advent of affordable public transportation, young people like Jenny Nuñez could travel from Pasadena to the beach. Jenny, now distanced from her birth name Juana, is at the beach smiling boldly in striped swimsuit and bobbed hair. (Daniel and Stella Castro Collection.)

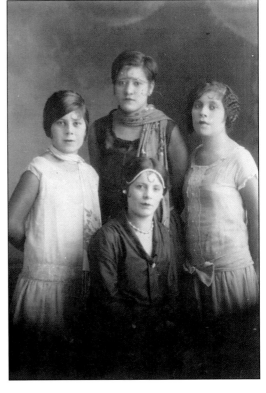

Integration of American ideals, if not integration of individuals, more and more began to be a part of Mexican and Mexican American youths and their experiences. Many who lived in the Sonora barrio, the *colonia* Chihuahuita, and the neighborhood of Winona-Cypress readily accepted the idea of the flapper. They may have heard the music of Al Jolson, Sousa marches, and Lydia Mendoza on the Victrola or radio. (Guerrero Collection.)

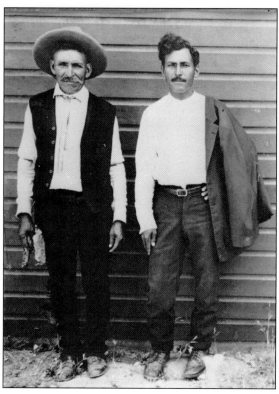

As people migrated west or north, it was not uncommon to have individuals acting as scouts. Daniel Berry formally served this role for the Indiana Colony. Similarly, individuals like Caterino Dominguez, pictured here to the left of his nephew Angel Contreras, filled this role for many who came from Mexico to Pasadena. Caterino may have come to the United States independently or may have been brought by Collis Huntington from Mexico to work on the railroads. The chart below is taken from Christine Lofstedt's thesis and presents information regarding immigrant point of origin in Mexico and duration of residence in Pasadena. (Both, Contreras Collection.)

TABLE II.

Birthplace	Chihuahuita	Northern Section	Southern Section	Total	Percent
Aguascalientes	10	24	33	67	8
Chihuahua	37	38	99	174	18
Coahuila	1	9	19	29	3
Colima	0	0	1	1	-
Durango	18	24	96	138	15
Guanajuato	1	23	20	44	5
Hidalgo	0	1	1	2	-
Jalisco	10	18	116	144	15
Lower California	0	5	11	16	2
Mexico City	5	8	12	25	3
Michoacan	0	9	30	39	4
Nuevo Leon	4	1	0	5	-
Pueble	1	0	1	2	-
San Luis Potosi	5	2	4	11	1
Sinaloa	6	0	9	15	1
Senora	11	19	35	65	7
Tabasco	0	0	1	1	-
Zacatecas	42	13	89	144	15
Somewhere in Mexico	7	13	5	25	3
TOTAL	158	207	582	947	100

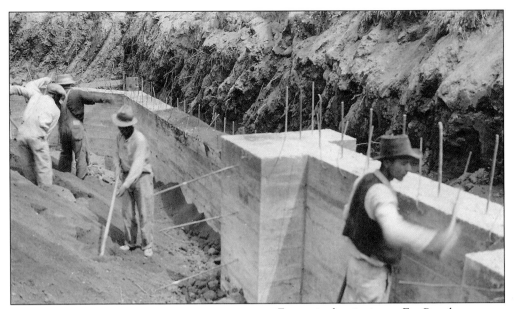

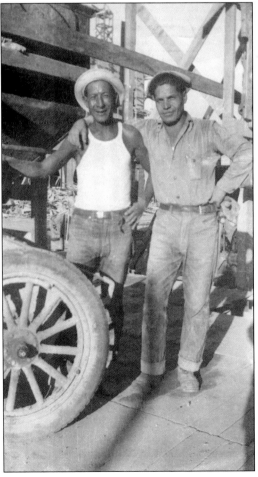

Every city has its icons. For Pasadena, it may be city hall, the Rose Bowl, or perhaps the Civic Auditorium. Each site benefitted from the architect's plan and from the construction workers' labor, which brought the work from vision to reality. Individuals from Latino and other working communities dug ditches, poured concrete, and added finishing touches, so others could enjoy the fruit of their labors. While many pictures exist focused on architects, administrators, and supervisors, there are few images that include the faces of those who daily toiled on civic projects. The names of those pictured working on city hall above are unidentified. The image at left of Jesus "Jess" Meza and his friend Esso at the Civic Auditorium shows that the work may have been humble but the pride was great; after all, this was their home. (Above, Pasadena Public Library; At left, Pasadena Museum of History.) [Civic Auditorium - Jess and Esso.]

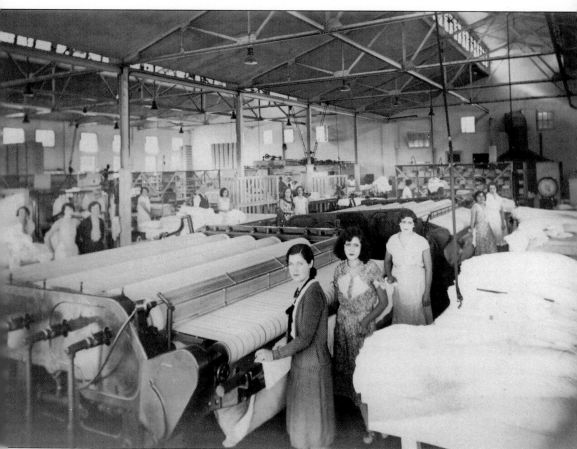

There was also great activity south of Colorado Street. In 1911, Our Lady of Guadalupe Mission Church was built, the labor being donated by the local parishioners. Following its erection, at what was to become Raymond Avenue and California Street, congregants came from as far away as Chihuahuita. Over time, the Union Mutualista de San José, La Apostolada, and Las Guadalupanas developed. The Union Mutualista was a mutual aid society. At what became Fillmore Street and Arroyo Parkway, the Reverend Francisco Olazabal, working in concert with those inspired by the Social Gospel Movement, raised thousands of dollars to build a mission-style church, the Iglesia Mexicana Metodista. Among programs developed by Reverend Olazabal was the Bonita Cooperative Laundry. This and other laundries allowed women to work at a site rather than traveling to individual homes. It was seen as a way to increase their family income for the home, was in keeping with traditional roles, and allowed for community interaction on the job. The site of this company photograph may have been the Home Laundry. (Guerrero Collection.)

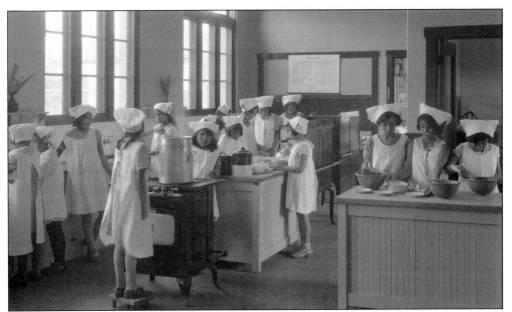

The "Report of Committee of Pasadena Council of Parents and Teachers Subject School Costs March 1932" revealed, "Three elementary schools offer part time economics courses. . . . These schools are for foreign born children who will not continue their education through the high school. The foods classes there prepare the school lunch, which furnishes a practical problem in larger quantity cookery." Pictured are fourth graders at Junipero Serra School preparing food for the school. (Pasadena Museum of History.)

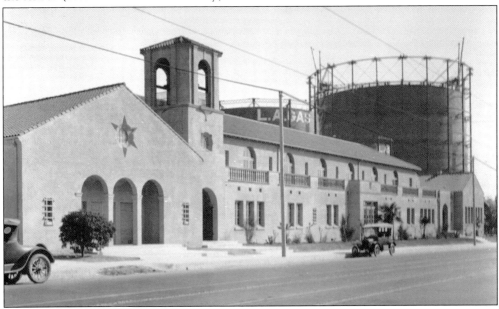

A former student referred to the school built in Southern Pasadena as "built strictly for Mexican children," and so it was. Progressive community members felt there was logic to building a school that would serve the needs of the children living in the area. Others appreciated Mexican children staying in their own neighborhoods. This is the second building that housed Junipero Serra School, closed in 1932 citing declining enrollment. (Pasadena Museum of History.)

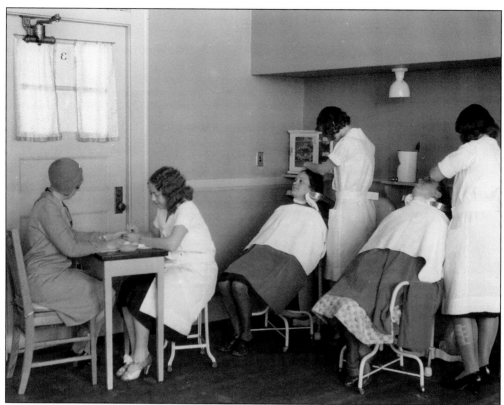

Young Mexican Americans emulated their screen idols. Men wanted to look like Rudolph Valentino or Ramon Novarro. A fashionable suit, a close shave, and some stylish shoes could do the trick. Women emulated Gloria Swanson or Mary Pickford. That meant time and teaching spent on manicures, eyebrow plucking, and Marcelle waves. John Muir High School developed a beauty trade class for beauty specialists who could fill that need. (Los Angeles Public Library.)

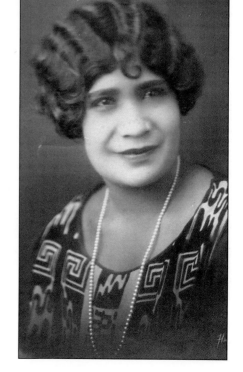

Jenny Nuñez Magdaleno shares her smile and her style in this photograph. Her hair is done in fine fashion, and her pearls complement the geometric design of her bodice, which may have been inspired by fashion's nod to either Aztec or Greek design. (Daniel and Stella Castro Collection.)

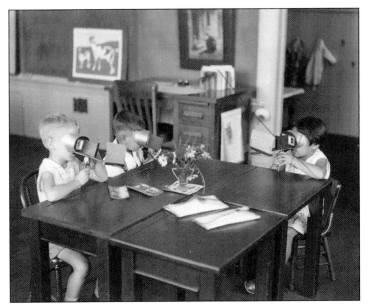

There are several possible reasons this photograph is marked as it is for cropping. The first and least visually satisfying answer has to do with the direction the children are facing. The large "X" on the dark-haired child belies that choice and is visually jarring. It was not uncommon as recently as the early 1970s to have photograph studios excise individuals based on ethnicity and race. (Pasadena Museum of History.)

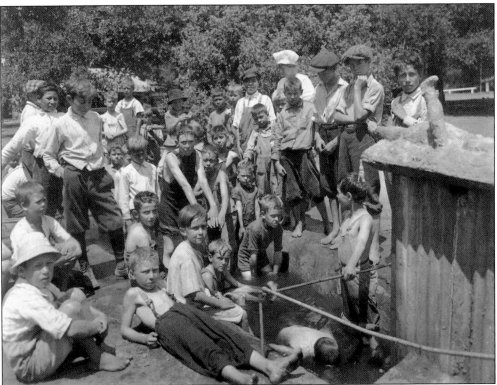

Boys who were anemic and pre-tubercular attended the Preventorium, established in 1922. The Pasadena Board of Education provided administrators and some teachers, and the rest of the needs were met by donations from community members. According to a "Report of Pasadena Council of Parents and Teachers Subject School costs March 1932," these were "services among children for whom the community should feel the greatest sense of responsibility." (Pasadena Museum of History.)

Manuel Pineda was born in Mexico in 1908 and brought to the United States as an infant. His family had been financially secure in Mexico but left because of interactions with Mexican revolutionaries. His father worked on the Rose Bowl in Pasadena. In order to stay in school, Manny sold newspapers and did other odd jobs. He graduated from Serra School, attended Muir School, and graduated from Pasadena High School in 1929. (Segura Collection.)

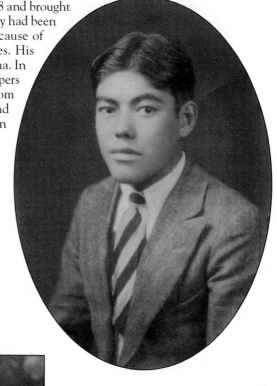

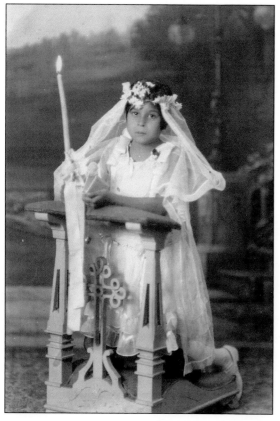

With migration and immigration came the separation of family members. Commemorations of social and religious ceremonies were often shared via photographs or photo postcards. Translated, the back of the photograph reads, "June 26, 1928. El Paso, Texas. I dedicate this humble memory of my first communion at the age of eight for you my Aunt Juana T. de Contreras your niece Gregoria Torres, present." (Contreras Collection.)

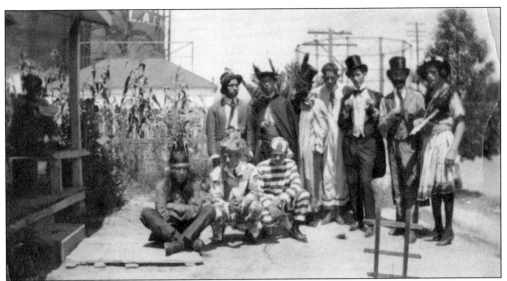

The Settlement Movement began in Chicago and focused on providing social betterment by a variety of means. Seeing similar needs in Pasadena, civic-minded citizens started a Settlement House in Pasadena's southern, commercial section. Alternately referred to as the Pasadena, Mexican, or Edna P. Alter Settlement, it provided a loan chest in case of illness, a Maternity Hospital, and a secondhand store. Classes included traditional folk expressions, English, "Americanization," and it was a good place to celebrate Halloween. (Pasadena Museum of History.)

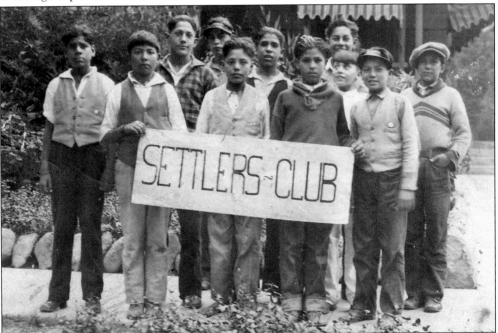

At the Settlement, a variety of clubs were established, each with the goal of keeping youngsters involved in positive rather than negative activities. National groups like Boy Scouts or Campfire Girls and groups that originated at the Settlement like "Settlers Club" and later the "Settlequeens" provided an opportunity for young people to spend time together and enjoy classes and field trips while in a safe environment. (Lopez/Mares Collection.)

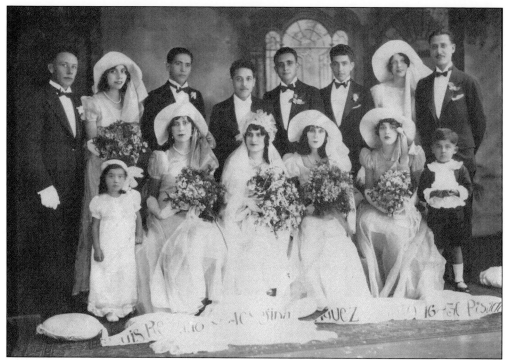

There were times when all community members came together. The larger, more formal wedding party became more traditional. Formal portraits memorialized this special day for the couple, the *compadres*, and the rest of the *familia*. Irene Enriquez is seated at the far right in the image above and is standing to the far left in the image below. The gowns' details display an amazing talent done with needle or sewing machine. (Both, Lopez/Mares Collection.)

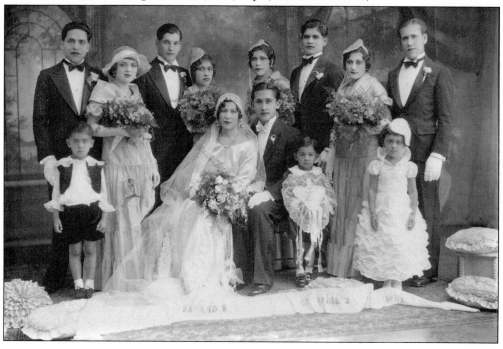

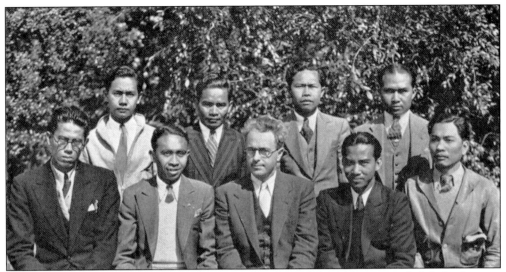

Pasadena Junior College had restricted and unrestricted clubs. The restricted clubs had names or a purpose that were generally abstract or symbolic. La Filipina Club's purpose was clear, direct, and touching. The quote for 1929 reads, "La Filipina touches the Filipino's heart as a reminder of home." From 1933, it reads, "Filipino students, coming to school in a strange land, find their longings for home and fellow-countrymen alleviated in the companionship of La Filipina." (Pasadena Museum of History.)

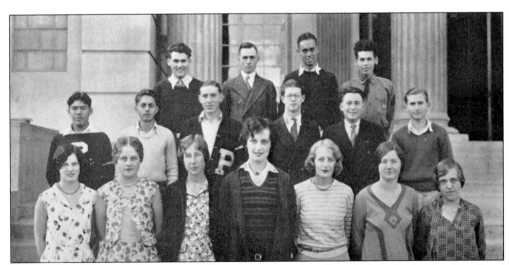

Manny Pineda was a school correspondent for the *Pasadena Post* while in high school, majored in journalism at Pasadena Junior College, and worked at the *Pasadena Post* before he graduated. He stayed on staff when the *Star News* bought the *Post*. He was the first Mexican sportswriter for the *Star News* and wrote *Pasadena Area History*, which is often praised for the caliber of the research and of the writing. (Pasadena Museum of History.)

Six

COMINGS AND GOINGS

At the beginning of the Great Depression in 1929, Mexican immigrants and native-born Americans of Mexican descent lived together in Pasadena. By 1931, many were deported to Mexico. Junipero Serra School closed because of declining enrollment; it is not recorded if these might have been children whose families were repatriated to Mexico. The Pasadena School District had established a 6-4-4 program, in which students were in elementary school for six years, a middle school for four years, and then two final years of high school, with the opportunity to attend college classes at the same campus. Some who remained in Pasadena were among the first graduating classes. The Settlement, which by this time had connections with the Maternity Hospital, Broadway Court, and a variety of clubs, was the hub of their lives. Pres. Franklin Delano Roosevelt, in an effort to develop jobs, established the Civilian Conservation Corps (CCC) to provide "simple work, not interfering with normal employment, and confining itself to forestry, the prevention of soil erosion, flood control, and similar projects." Another program, the Works Progress Administration, paid for the translation of early California documents. The Pasadena Playhouse was designated the Official State Theatre of California in 1937. Gilmor Brown, one of its cofounders, focused its Midsummer Festival on the "Story of the Great Southwest." Actors and performers included Mingo Vasquez, Felix Gutierrez, and Nati Vacio—all from Chihuahuita. The Tournament of Roses continued to highlight the Californio experience; in 1937, sheriff Eugene W. Biscailuz was grand marshal. The United States' response to World War II altered the work and the future of many Mexican Americans. Men, residents, and non-residents alike, were drafted into service. Women, who stayed behind, began to experience the evolution of identity and roles, as they worked shoulder to shoulder with women from different cultures and heritages. Working in factories, be they canneries or airplane factories, changed the sense of women's capabilities. With American men fighting overseas, workers from Mexico were brought to the United States via the Bracero Program.

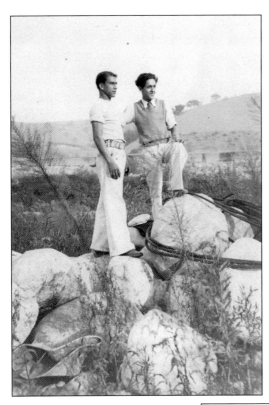

In the early 1930s, the box camera became popular. It allowed for a portability that had not existed before. Pictures like this of Jesus and Gregorio Enriquez in the Arroyo, or Jess and George (in vest), as their friends called them, became more common. A moment in the Arroyo became something that could be easily shared with friends and family, near or far. (Lopez/Mares Collection.)

Danny Castro came from El Paso, Texas, to Pasadena, California, in 1934 and was among those who were in the CCC. Many worked in city parks, state parks, and national parks on buildings, trails, archaeological excavation, and the construction of logging and fire roads. In this case, Danny came, worked at Oak Grove, and stayed in Pasadena. (Daniel and Stella Castro Collection.)

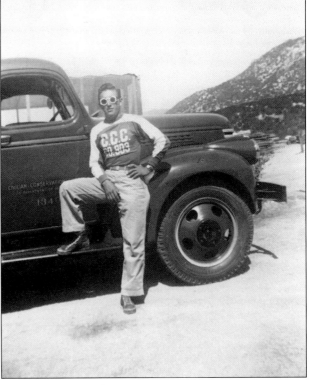

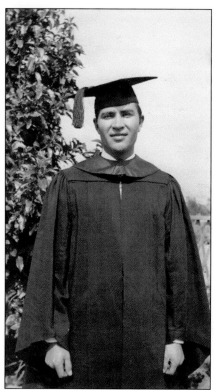

Natividad "Nati" Vacio came with his family to Chihuahuita in 1923. Nati graduated from Pasadena Junior College in 1934 and later earned his teaching credential. As a part of the "Comedia del Arte" at Padua Hills in Claremont, Nati developed skills as a musician, dancer, producer, and director, which he used in his work in Pasadena at the Mexican Settlement. In 1937, Gilmor Brown, of the Pasadena Playhouse, presented a festival highlighting the great Southwest; Nati was among the local talents hired. Later his friend George Reeves introduced him to a director who permitted Nati to come to work after he finished teaching school. He performed on screen, stage, and television, ever proud of his roots in Chihuahuita. Among his last appearances was *The Milagro Beanfield War*, produced by Moctezuma Esparza and directed by Robert Redford. Nati is standing center in the photograph below. (Both, Contreras Collection.)

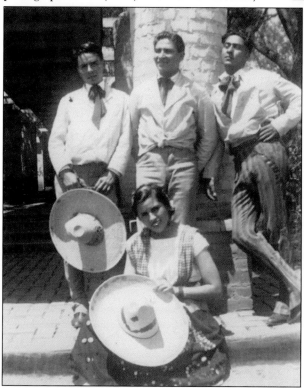

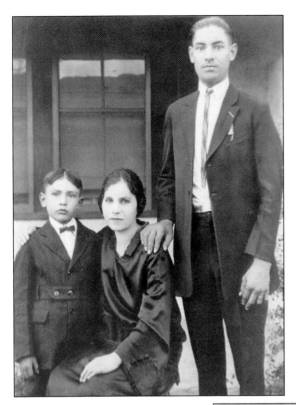

Broadway Court, located in the commercial, southern section of Pasadena, was built for Mexican families. It was a significant pioneer effort in affordable housing. Dressed in their finery, this family poses, looking proud and pleased. Prior substandard housing had been condemned by the city. (Guerrero Collection.)

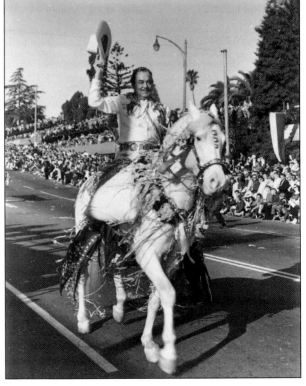

Leo Carrillo was the Tournament of Roses grand marshal in 1938. He was an actor, political cartoonist, and conservationist, serving on the California Commission for Beaches and Parks for 18 years. He was proud of his family's heritage and history, which included a governor of Alta California and a mayor of Los Angeles. Carrillo appeared in films and on television; he was best known as "Pancho" on *The Cisco Kid*. (Pasadena Tournament of Roses Archives.)

Brought on in part by the Depression, the repatriation of *Mexicanos* and their families took place beginning in 1929. Of the estimated one million repatriated nationwide, approximately 60 percent were American citizens. Over 100 people left Pasadena in April 1931. Johnny and his big brother, Manny Contreras, remained in Pasadena and, like most children, were more concerned about how well the "wagon" would steer than the larger political and social changes. (Contreras Collection.)

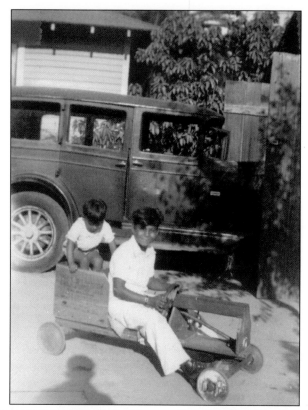

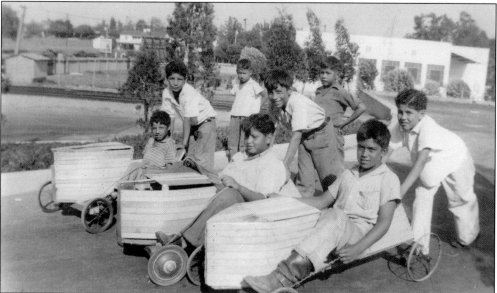

Lack of money during the 1930s and rationing during the war years limited the kinds and amounts of toys children played with, so creativity became a part of many a child's toolset. Mauricio "Wicho" Valadez (center), with his winning smile, and friends lived near Raymond Hill. They made the smooth aerodynamic curves on their "wagons" by using lathing, which had been soaked and then formed to fit their frames; hubcaps or boots with buckles were optional. (Valadez Collection.)

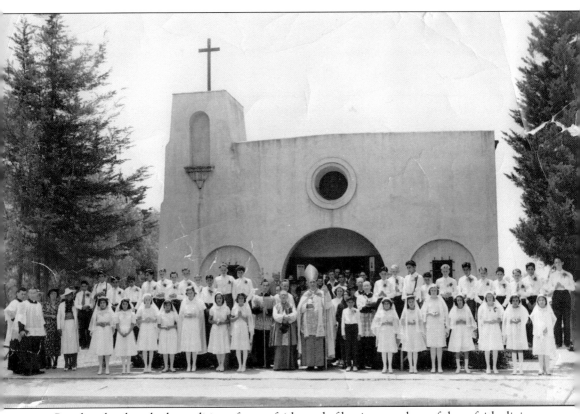

Pasadena has long had a tradition of many faiths and of having members of those faiths living as neighbors. In Chihuahuita, a Methodist church and Roman Catholic church were on the same block. While elders at both houses of worship may have been determined on keeping, or gaining, members of the flock, the focus and the experiences of the children were very different. Seniors remembering their youth speak of going to the Methodist church for hot chocolate on Wednesday and going to the Catholic *jamaicas*, or fiestas, when they took place. This is a photograph of a confirmation at Sacred Heart Catholic Church when it was on the corner of Washington Boulevard and Lincoln Avenue. (Estrada Collection.)

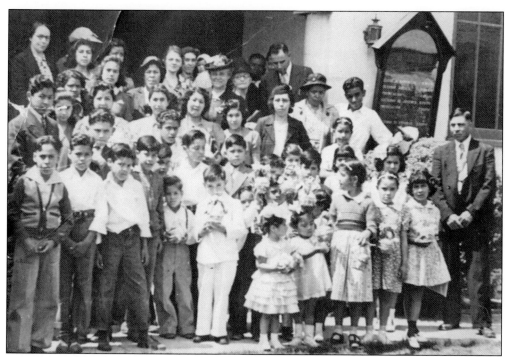

Although the Roman Catholic churches had the largest congregations in the Mexican communities in Pasadena, there were other churches of significant size. Both the Pasadena Nazarene Church (above) and the Iglesia Metodista Mexicana (below), as it was commonly known, had large congregations. Members of the Lopez family were congregants of Iglesia Metodista Mexicana. The photograph below was taken on Easter Sunday and shows about a third of the congregation in the original picture. (Above, Pasadena Museum of History; below, Segura Collection.)

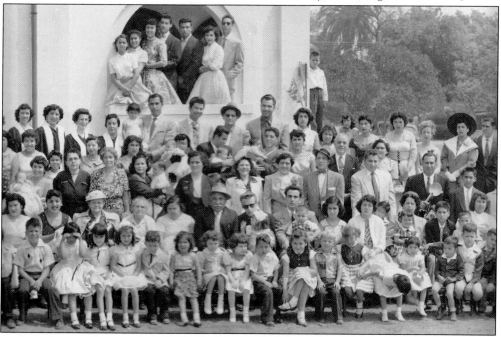

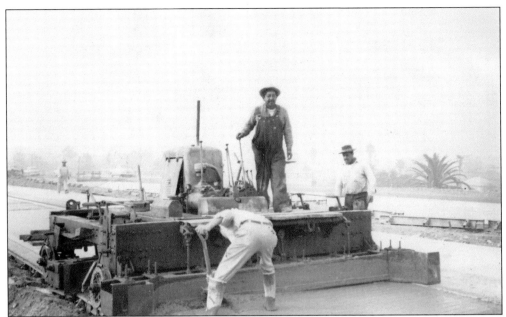

Tony Magdaleno of Pasadena operates a machine laying asphalt covering the width of the future lanes of the Arroyo Seco Freeway. Its construction was begun in 1938 in response to the growing numbers of people traveling between Pasadena and Los Angeles. It became the first freeway in Southern California. Magdaleno was an early member of the Operating Engineers Union. (Daniel and Stella Castro Collection.)

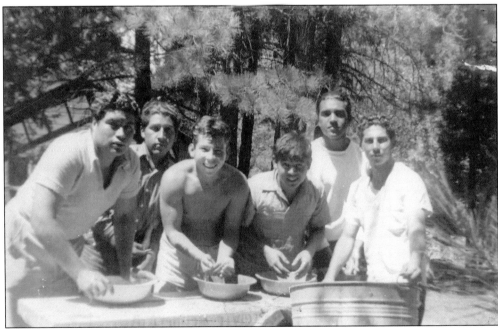

These Boy Scouts in 1939 look pretty much like Scouts one would see today. This troop had its origins at the Pasadena Settlement. According to Manny Pineda, he "went through" three times and then gave up because each year they had a new leader and they had to start all over again. The Scouts here seem focused on having fun. (Contreras Collection.)

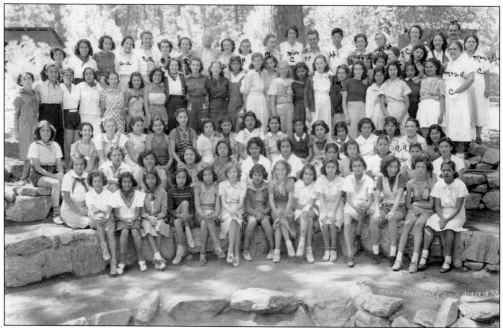

The idea of girls attending a camp without family would not have been easily accepted during the first quarter of the 20th century. By the late 1930s, this idea was acceptable and welcomed by the girls and most of their parents. Girls also were more likely to continue attending school through high school. Mexican girls at Camp Arata are shown above in 1937. Stella Nuñez is seated fourth from the right in this picture taken at McKinley School. (Above, Segura Collection; below, Daniel and Stella Castro Collection.)

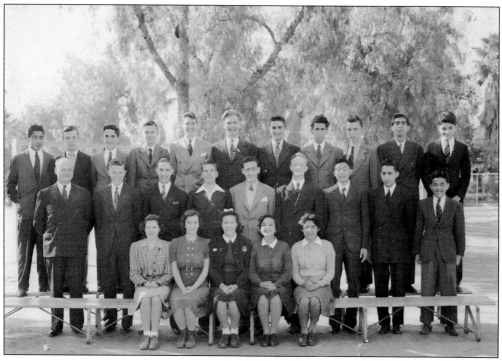

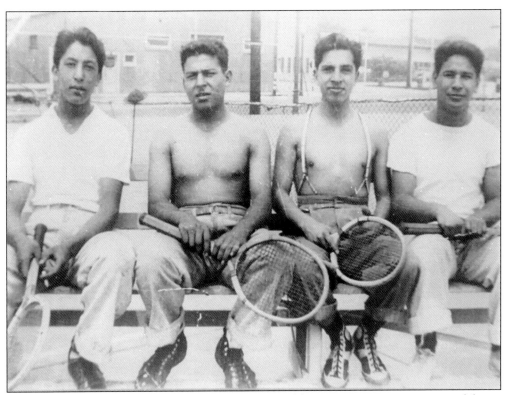

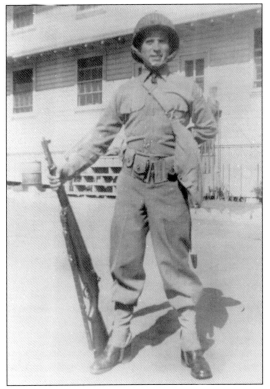

Athletics were an important part of the lives of young men. Pictured above, from left to right, are Frank Ituarde, Ernest Solario, Fernando Mendias, and Santos Rodriguez. They knew all about the all-American games of basketball, baseball, and tennis. They were also cognizant of the sundown "rule," which meant that they were to be off the streets and home by sunset. *Mendez v. Westminster* began to bring an end in segregation based on national origin. (Pasadena Mexican American History Association.)

Joe Jaramillo was killed in Italy. He was one of nearly 400,000 Mexican Americans who served during World War II. Although many died, none were tried for desertion or treason; many soldiers returned and developed self-assistance groups like American GI Forum and Uni-Vets. Having been willing to give their life for their country, they felt they should have opportunities and rights equal to anyone else in the country. (Pasadena Mexican American History Association.)

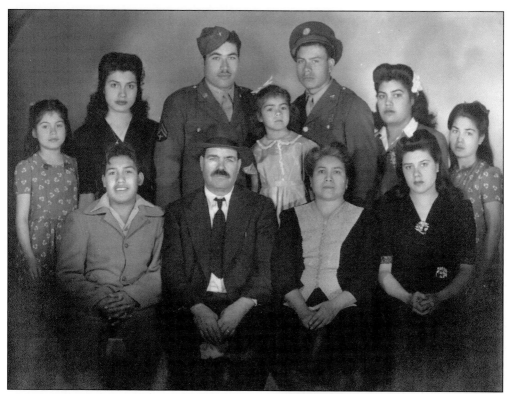

This formal portrait could be of any family that had sons and daughters the same age during World War ll. Mr. and Mrs. Valadez seem to bear witness to the gravity that war can bring, their sons each have their own response to the future, the older sisters are wearing their "Victory Rolls," and the youngest sister leans on one of her big brothers. (Valadez Collection.)

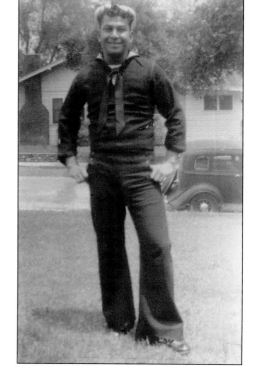

Manny Contreras stands proudly in his Coast Guard uniform. He and others who were not at the front line felt they too were making their contributions to the war effort by transporting goods, working in factories, canning and rationing food, raising victory gardens, working in industries that offered direct support, or by keeping the home front ready for the return of "the Boys." (Contreras Collection.)

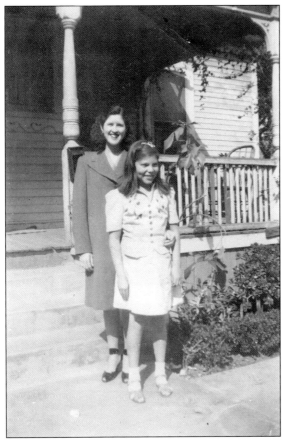

Belen Lopez's parents attended Pasadena schools, met, and married in Pasadena. The Lopez family was repatriated and lived in the state of Chihuahua, Mexico, from 1931 to 1934. While they were in Mexico, a brother was born. A sister died and was buried in Mexico. They left Pasadena because they were promised land in Mexico, but the land they were given was not good for growing crops. Belen was conceived in Mexico and was born in the United States in January 1935. Belen easily interacted with those she knew who were a part of life in Pasadena and with those who were a part of her family's life in Mexico. Belen, like other children growing up at this time, felt comfortable with both American friends and Mexican *familia*. Sometimes the friends and *familia* did not know each other. Belen is pictured with cousin Concha (above) and best friend Faithie (below). (Both, Segura Collection.)

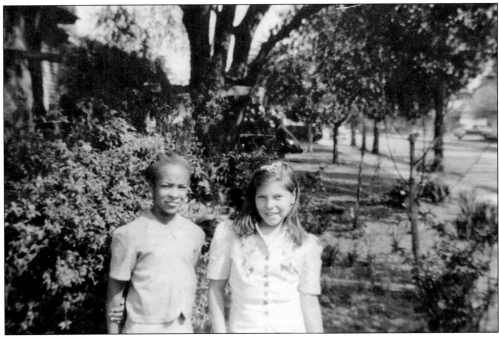

Seven

FINDING OUR VOICE

In June 1943, the Zoot Suit Riots occurred. The response to the violent interaction between military personnel and Mexican Americans was varied. The Xochimilco Club at Pasadena Junior College seemed to allude to existing tensions in its statement of purpose:

> The purpose . . . will be to promote cultural, social, and recreational activities and to encourage more participation in other club activities offered by the school among the students of Mexican, Spanish, or other Latin American ancestries enrolled at Pasadena Junior College. . . . Racial problems are discussed at meetings of the group, its members attempting to decrease racial prejudice . . . thereby promoting good will among students of different nationalities.

Some of the group's officers, such as Jessie Magdaleno, Vivian Dominguez, Manny Contreras, and Mauricio Valadez, continued to be involved with groups focused on education, identity, and interaction among different groups throughout their lives. Club member Socorro Singh's family was very likely from the Central Valley. Young men who were Sikhs came to the valley to work, and because of anti-miscegenation laws they could only marry nonwhite women. Discrimination and segregation that had been accepted, or at least tolerated, before World War II was not easily accepted by returning soldiers. They had been to war, seen friends and loved ones killed, and perhaps had killed enemies protecting the rights of their country. In Orange County, Gonzalo Mendez sued Westminster School District, claiming he and his family were victims of unconstitutional discrimination. They won their appellate case with *amicus curiae*, including the National Association for Colored People, the Anti-Defamation League, Japanese American Citizens League, and the League of United American Citizens, among others. Legal strategy developed by Thurgood Marshall, presented in the NAACP amicus brief, was precedent to *Brown v. Board of Education*. Returning soldiers used the Servicemen's Readjustment Act of 1944 (GI Bill) for college or vocational education and took advantage of loans to buy homes or start businesses. The arrival of Stephen A. Reyes strengthened efforts focused on community building and educational attainment. He was one of the founders of the Pasadena Scholarship Committee.

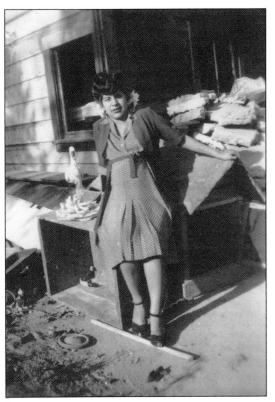

No longer standing on a chair, Stella Nuñez Castro appears ready to meet her future. She attended Fremont Elementary School and lived for a while in Chihuahuita. She is posed and poised looking very "smooth" in contrast to the rough-hewn building behind her. The bird in this picture is a stork, perhaps a token from a baby shower. (Daniel and Stella Castro Collection.)

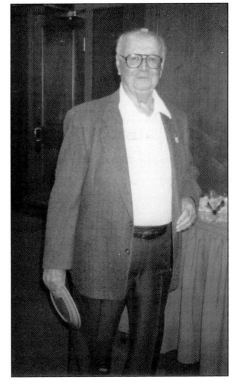

Manny Perez grew up in Chihuahuita and as a young child met Albert Einstein. He went against advice to change his name to Perry "because he didn't look Mexican." Perez it stayed, while he was in the service, attended Occidental College and the University of Southern California, and when he became the first Mexican American teacher in Pasadena School District in 1958 and the first Mexican American dean at Pasadena City College in 1971. (Contreras Collection.)

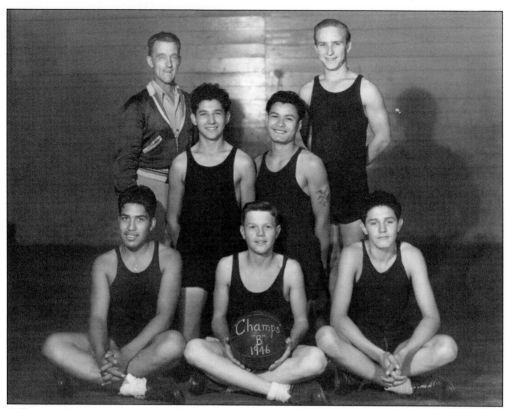

Following the war, many organizations became more integrated, and many young people in Pasadena began to assume this was a good and natural thing. While many still lived in neighborhoods where their neighbors shared common ancestry, interacting with others became more common at places like the Boys Club, as this picture taken in 1946 shows. (Valadez Collection.)

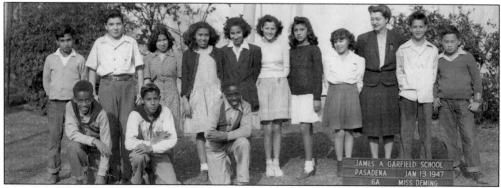

This 1947 image of Garfield Elementary includes a classmate Johnnie Sogi, who was not in class pictures during the war years. The internment of Japanese Americans saddened many neighbors living in the Wynona/Cypress area of Pasadena. Seniors speak of the tears shared by them and black neighbors when their Japanese American neighbors left. Some share the guilt they felt because their families bought homes left by their neighbors. (Segura Collection.)

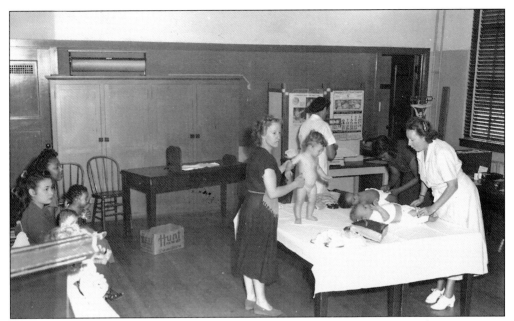

The Pasadena City Health Department held this Well Baby Clinic in 1949. This service was generally directed to those who could not afford a family doctor, often providing immunizations for childhood diseases. The City of Pasadena had been providing health services since the 1920s to Mexican Americans living in southern Pasadena and also to those in Chihuahuita, despite the fact it was not within city boundaries. (Pasadena Public Library.)

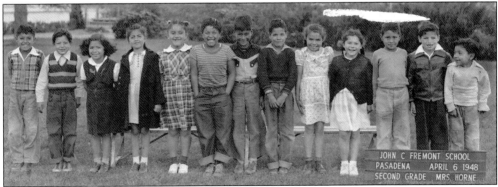

Roger Mejia is standing third from the right in this 1948 Fremont Elementary class photograph. Roger remembers that the old Fremont building had showers, and their use was free, "so you would see people going there with their towels and their clothes." His father worked on the railroad, picked oranges in Pasadena, and worked for the City of Pasadena. In 1969, his family started El Ranchero Restaurant; some employees have worked there for over 30 years. (Mejia Collection.)

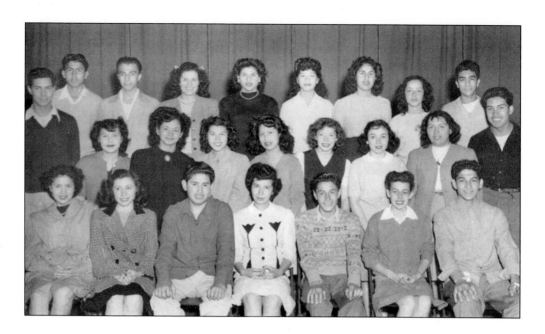

In 1947, the Xochimilco Club at Pasadena Junior College stated that its "purpose of the organization is to further the ideals of racial equality. Besides social events, topic meetings are held to discuss racial problems, the purpose being to try to decrease racial prejudice. Members strive to offer participation all campus activities and thereby insure greater cooperation and understanding among P.J.C. students of different nationalities." The group's advisor, with the dapper moustache (below, far right), is Stephen Reyes. Born in Etiwanda, he worked the fields with his family and began kindergarten at age eight with no English. At 15, he lost his arm in a hunting accident. At 16, he was ready to quit school, but a foreman encouraged him to stay. With determination, he earned an associate's degree from PJC, a bachelor of arts from UCLA in 1938, and a master of arts from USC in 1948. He began work at the Pasadena Settlement in 1938, and as a result, participation rose dramatically. For the next four decades, he organized or founded organizations at both the local and statewide levels. (Both, Pasadena Museum of History.)

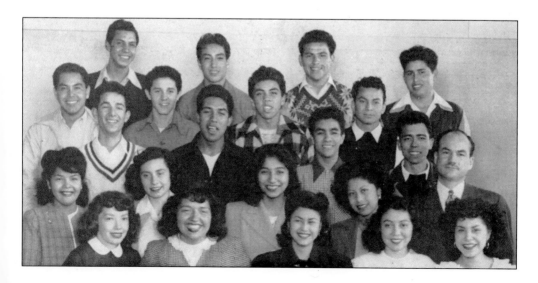

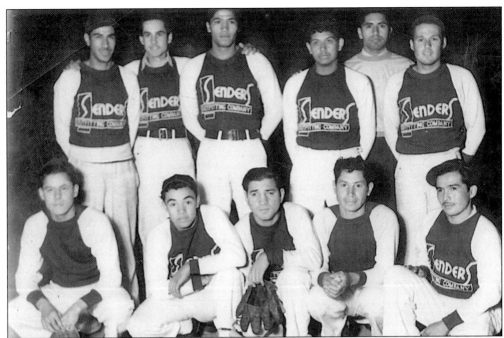

The lives of Canto Robledo and Maria Luisa Mitchell were very different from each other. Canto (above) grew up in New Mexico, came with his family to California, worked in the fields, and then turned to boxing as both a passion and a way to make a livelihood. Maria Luisa (below) grew up in Pasadena, graduated from St. Andrew's High School, and gradually became a community activist. Their common experience was overcoming a physical limitation and contributing to the community in many ways. Canto (front row center), after being blinded, became a trainer of boxers in northwest Pasadena. He also coached baseball, using the information from assistant coaches in developing plans for team players. Maria Luisa, after battling polio as a child, became actively involved with the educational and social changes in the school district in the late 1960s. Both shared determination and a willingness to work toward a goal, whether it was winning a contest of ability and strength or challenging the status quo. (Above, Robledo Collection; below, Isenberg Collection.)

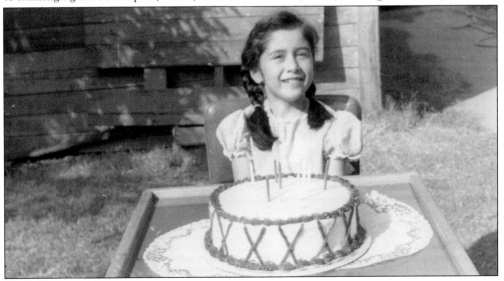

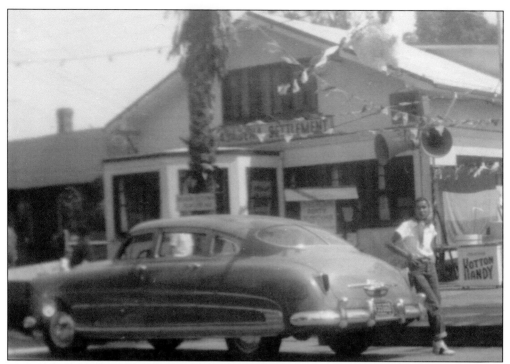

The Settlement function, name, and site changed over the years. After World War II, the building and organization was moved to Del Mar Avenue. This picture was taken prior to a special event at the Settlement in 1951, perhaps a *jamaica*. During a *jamaica*, or community fair, each club would take the lead on an activity. The women typically would prepare food, and the men would construct the booths. (Contreras Collection.)

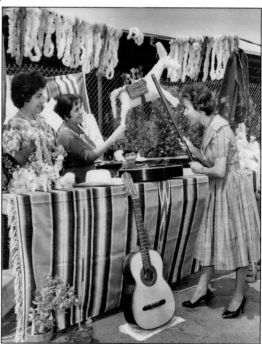

The word *jamaica* comes from the Arawak language. "*Xaymaca*" or "*Xamaika*" means land of wood and water. Over time, it has come to mean an island nation, a drink made from the hibiscus flower, and, beginning in 18th-century Mexico, a community fair. For years, churches have held *jamaicas* as a means of raising money. From left to right are Stella Castro, Sally Ruiz, and Maxine Casso as they prepare for a *jamaica* in Pasadena. (Daniel and Stella Castro Collection.)

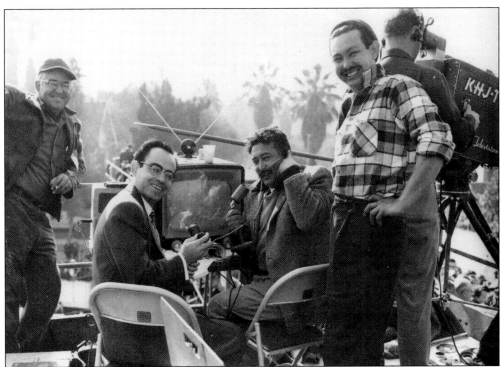

Ted Fregoso, Eddie Rodriguez (seated), and Pete Rodriguez (standing) have been involved with English- and Spanish-speaking media and broadcasting from the late 1940s through the 21st century. This photograph was taken on January 1, 1952, during the first television and radio simulcast of the Tournament of Roses Parade. According to Fregoso, they had a great view from their station balcony at 756 East Colorado Boulevard in Pasadena. (Security Pacific Collection/ Los Angeles Public Library.)

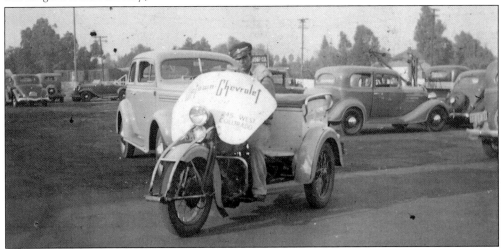

Jess Lopez was 26 years old and working at Uptown Chevrolet when his first daughter, Jeanette Joyce, was born to him and Irene Enriquez Lopez. The Lopez family lived on Dayton Street and then on Bellevue Street, in the southern section of Pasadena, while he was working with Uptown. He was a parts man and worked for Chevrolet (at different sites) for approximately 47 years. (Lopez/Mares Collection.)

Many who had been involved with the Settlement continued organizing social groups or strengthening existing groups in Pasadena. Uni-Vets began somewhat informally in 1948 and continued until the 1990s. Primarily a social club, it organized an annual ball where a queen was crowned. In 1954, actor Ricardo Montalbán crowned the *Churubusco Reina*. (Contreras Collection.)

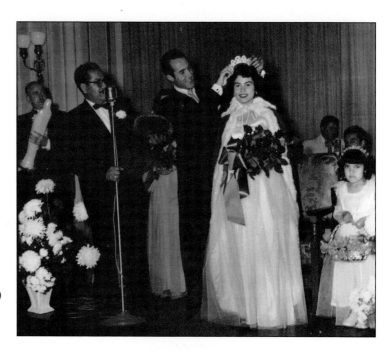

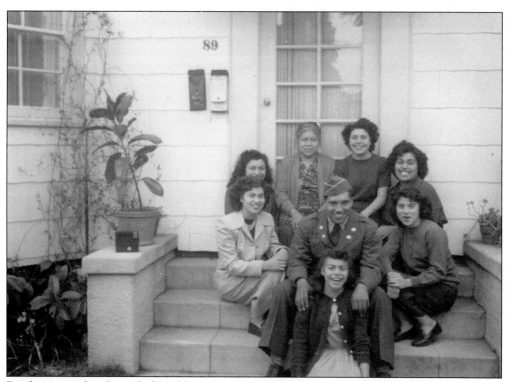

But five years after the end of World War II, young Mexican American men were again in uniform. The contrast of the photograph of Señora Valadez, her daughters, and her youngest son Mauricio ("Wicho") in uniform is radically different from the formal photograph taken of the family during World War II. (Valadez Collection.)

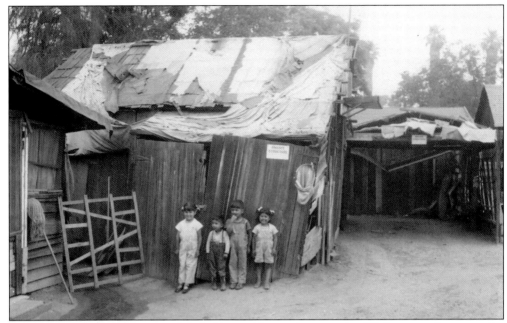

This image was found in an unlabeled box of loose photographs. With no markings on the photograph, one can only absorb the contrasting information in the picture. Here is a group of young children, carefully coiffed and neatly dressed, smiling broadly. They stand near the gate that had been set up, which sits on top of flowing water that almost touches the household mop.

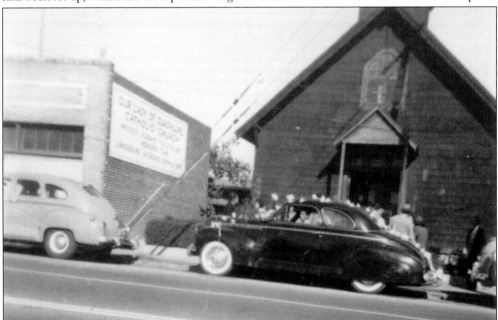

In 1911, Bishop James Conaty directed that a mission church be established to serve the Mexican population of the South Raymond Avenue area. In 1912, Our Lady of Guadalupe was built by the parishioners. It remained a center of religious, cultural, and social life for over five decades. It was one of the few places where *mandas*—promises of religious acts of devotion, made in thanksgiving— were made to Our Lady of Guadalupe. (Pasadena Museum of History.) (Estrada Collection.)

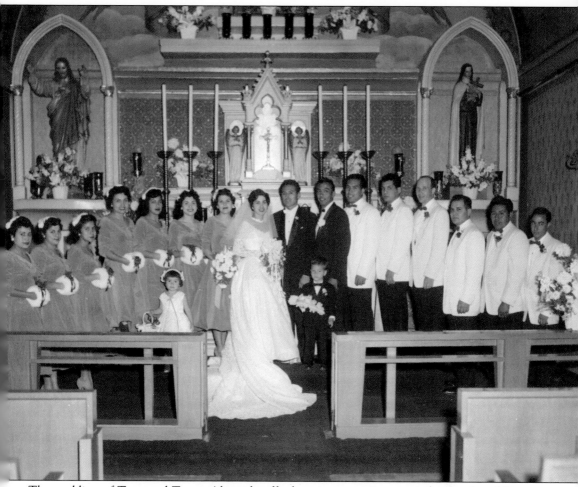

The wedding of Tony and Teresa Alvarado affords an opportunity to see the interior of Our Lady of Guadalupe. The church was small; the wedding party filled the width of the sanctuary. Not visible is the image of the *Virgen* above the altar, which can now be found at St. Andrew's Catholic Church on Raymond Avenue. (Valadez Collection.)

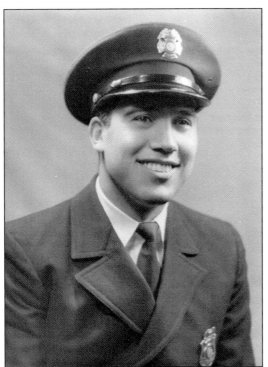

Every group has pioneers. Eugene F. Peron was perhaps the first Latino to serve on the Pasadena Police Department. There are others who have lived in Pasadena and were groundbreakers in other fields. Mauricio Valadez was the first Mexican American to serve in the Pasadena Fire Department. In this picture taken in uniform in 1956, one can see his great smile and guess his pride. (Valadez Collection.)

It is not known how many of the attendees in the picture were a part of the Filipino community in Pasadena. However, sitting in this posed picture are Gloria Ilejay and her younger brother Robert "Bobbie" Ilejay. Gloria was married to Sam Balucas, who later became the Los Angeles Chapter president of the Filipino American National Historical Society. (Security Pacific Collection/ Los Angeles Public Library.)

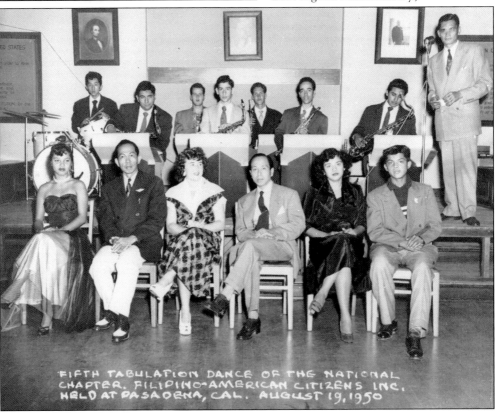

Names change to reflect their social context. Names that were common in Mexico were often modified or abbreviated once a family member had lived a long time in the United States. Here Tía Josefina "Chepa" Gonzales is arriving on a serious sewing mission. Tía Angie Gutierrez sits on the family porch holding Daniel "Danny" Estrada. (Estrada Collection.)

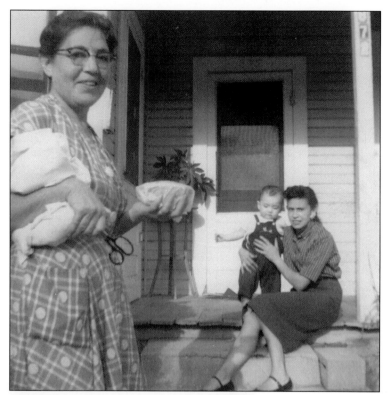

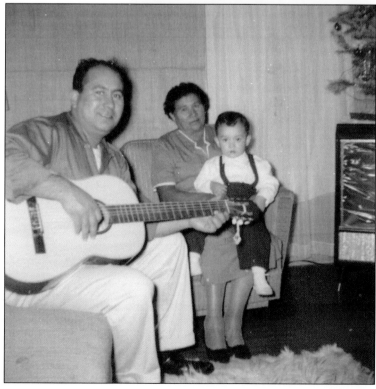

In the 1950s, it was not unusual for several members of a family to live within blocks of each other or to live some distance from each other, so visits were viewed as special times. This was in part a result of restrictive covenants, which would not permit other than white persons to live in certain areas. Little Danny and his father, Freddie, enjoy a visit with Grandma Carmen Estrada. (Estrada Collection.)

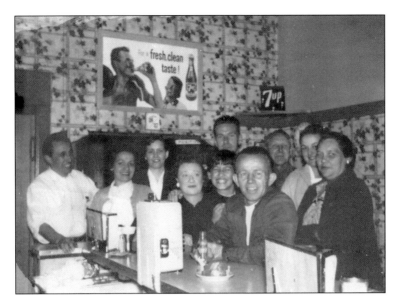

Danny Castro was always willing to try something new. Danny's Café was established in 1954. Located at the corner of Fair Oaks Avenue and Colorado Boulevard, the café was a place for all sorts of folks to gather in downtown Pasadena. Good food, good music, and good people meant having a real good time. (Collection of Daniel and Stella Castro.)

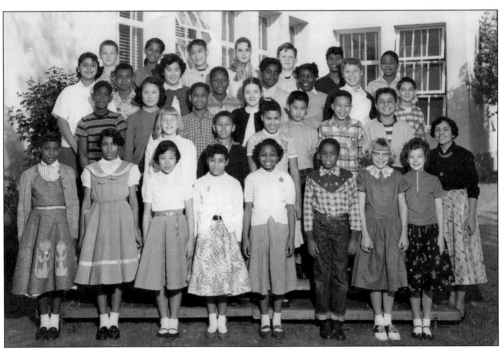

The children who attended Lincoln School lived in the Wynona/Cypress area of Pasadena. This class reflects a unique community in Pasadena's history. Many families in the area had parents with trades who had lived in their homes long enough to have some discretionary money. With the advent of the 210 Freeway, this established blue-collar community ceased to exist, its members becoming a small diaspora spread throughout the city. (Guerrero Collection.)

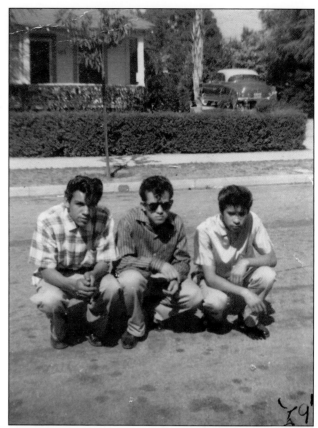

So often when we think of style, we automatically think of girls and women. Boys and men also express style as statement. From left to right are, Bobby, Eddie, and Alfonso who are making a statement that was probably far different from the fashion statements made by the older men in their family. Below, Manny Contreras, fifth from right, along with the other members of this wedding party were making their statement, too. (At right, Lopez/Mares; below, Contreras Collection.)

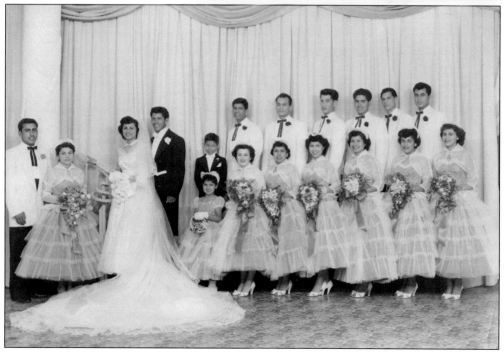

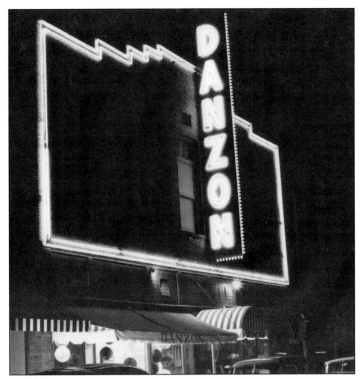

Danny Castro brought some *Tejano* bravura with him to Pasadena. In addition to working in the construction field, he established several businesses. Pasadena Transfer and Trucking Company, Danny's Café, and Fair Deal Realty were some of his ventures. Danzon was a unique venture in Pasadena. Danzon was a local nightclub, complete with dance floor and beautiful white grand piano. At times, the music was broadcast and Pasadenans like Pat Guerrero had a brief moment of fame as family members heard her on the radio. (Both, Daniel and Stella Castro Collection.)

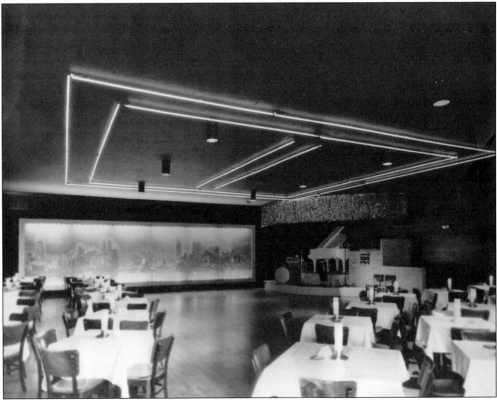

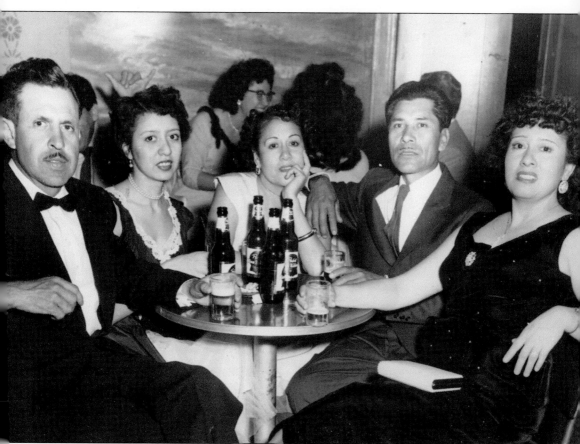

Following World War II, as the economy was rebuilding and industry was advancing, veterans and their families enjoyed evenings out on the town. Lalo's in East Los Angeles, owned by musician Lalo Guerrero, like Danzon in Pasadena, was a gathering spot for a good social time. Patrons listened to music that had Caribbean, Puerto Rican, and Cuban roots. Above are, from left to right, Joe Romero, Jenny Romero Jr., Ruth Guerrero, Jose Guerrero, and Jenny Romero. (Guerrero Collection.)

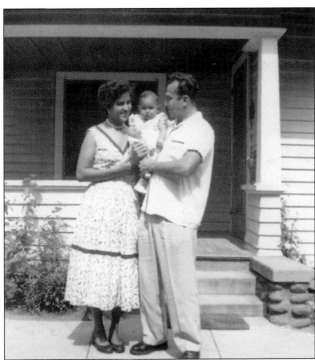

Many of the homes sprinkled throughout Pasadena were bungalows built during the 1920s and 1930s. The majority of these houses were modest in size, with yards that had room for gardens and clotheslines. Young families could furnish their homes and take care of their yards. Manny and Gertrude Contreras, like others who lived through the Depression and the war years, enjoyed a respite. (Contreras Collection.)

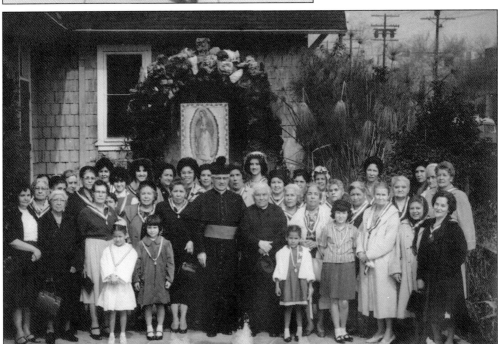

Las Guadalupanas, like other señoras, were the backbone of the community. They performed necessary work for the upkeep of the church and kept a sense of order, structure, and tradition in the community. Their prayers, their *remedios*, and even their language kept families connected with their heritage. Many became naturalized citizens in the 1950s. The United States had become their country, and they wanted their voice heard and vote counted. (Guerrero Collection.)

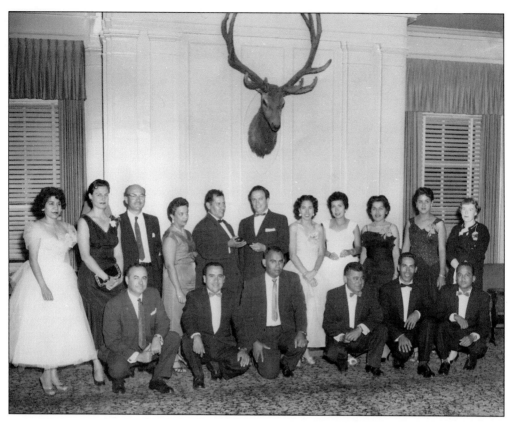

The Pasadena Scholarship Committee was established in 1954, originally dedicated exclusively for Mexican American students. Currently known as the Pasadena Scholarship Committee for Americans of Mexican and Latino Descent, it exists to inspire Latino high school seniors to pursue higher educations. Pasadena scholarship recipients are shown above, and the scholarship committee is below. (Above, Pasadena Mexican American History Association; below, Daniel and Stella Castro Collection.)

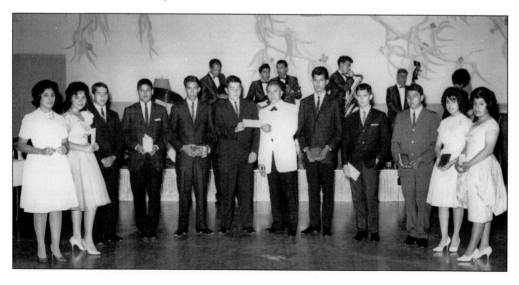

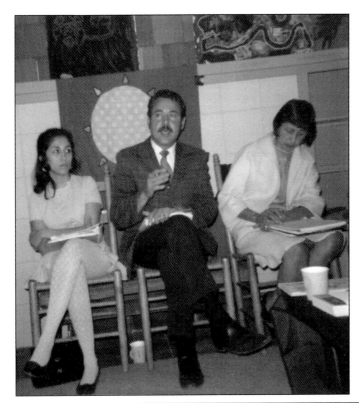

Throughout Elias Galvan's professional life, he remembered what it was like to be a child who entered school speaking no English. Like others, he married young, had children, and then worked to support his family. His positive collaborative attitude contributed to his becoming principal at Muir High School in 1971. He is here with Maria Luisa Isenberg (left) and Viviana Aparicio Chamberlin (right) talking and listening to community members at Pacific Oaks College. (Isenberg Collection.)

Daniel Castro and Nena Maynez decided to express their sense of identity at their wedding in 1971. The men dressed as *Charros*, and a serape with the image of the *Indigeno* from *La America Tropical* and mariachis were in the sacristy. When the priest at Our Lady of Guadalupe found this too radical, a friend, Fr. David Gomez, was the celebrant. (Daniel and Stella Castro Collection.)

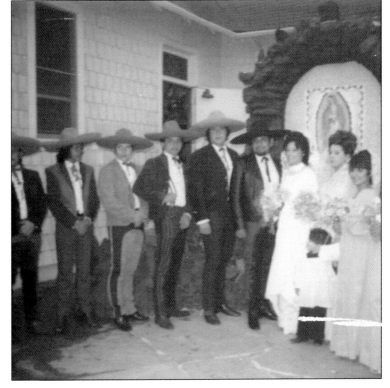

Eight

REDEFINING IDENTITY

From 1968 to 1980, the time it takes a child to go through school, there were huge changes in the world and in Pasadena. There was a questioning of the status quo—in Spanish-speaking countries, in France, in the United Kingdom, and in the United States. How people referred to themselves during this period told much about their political or social stance: about feelings regarding acculturation or assimilation, about feelings regarding identity and race, about their sense of the land that was their home. Many who felt ostracized and marginalized worked in collaboration for change, many identifying themselves as Chicanos. Much literature is available regarding the 1970 order to desegregate the Pasadena Unified Schools; the effect on the Chicano/ Mexican American community is not generally included. In addition, the Latino community lost three cultural anchors. The closing of the Pasadena Settlement was the loss of a central point of interaction for members of the community. A fire, which destroyed mission church Our Lady of Guadalupe, was a second blow to the community. "We have a love for Guadalupe Church, which outsiders cannot easily understand," said Alice Mijares. "I was baptized in that church, I had my first communion there, I was married there, and my children were baptized there." So beloved was the church that Andrea Gutierrez led a contingent to ask Pope John Paul II permission to rebuild it or convert it to a community center, with labor to be donated by congregants. The relocation of members from the Wynona/Cypress neighborhood when the 210 Freeway was built was a final blow. One family moving to Hastings Ranch neighborhood first dealt with the loss of their neighbors and then a Molotov cocktail thrown at their new home in 1978. Despite, or because of this, community pulled together and developed allies, a clear sense of direction, and political power to modify their opportunities and status. There were an increased number in the community who had advanced in education or in business. The Latino population in Pasadena increased from 10 percent in 1970 to 20 percent in 1980.

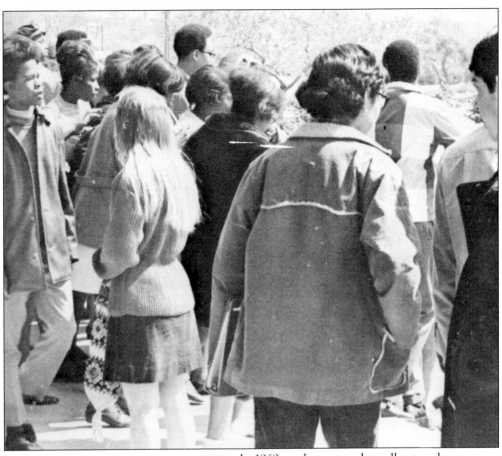

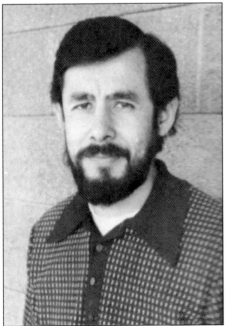

In 1969, students staged a walkout and a boycott in response to discriminatory practices at the three high schools; black students led the protests. According to Ed Maya (below), "Black leaders and students were voicing demands for 'all' minorities." The protests lasted for four days. Adults, administration, and the school board responded positively to the students' requests. The students felt their self-discipline and lack of violence had earned them "new dignity and respect." (Both, Pasadena Unified School District.)

Villa Parke Community Center, built on the site of a former boys' club and established in 1973, was renovated in the 1990s. The center, an early effort in walkable urban sites, provides services to approximately 18,000 client visits per month. Executive director Serafin Espinoza has been at this community center for 30 years. While all community members are welcome at the facility, the majority of clients are Latino and Spanish-dominant or bilingual. Recent immigrants see it as a port of entry, a place to learn what is expected of them in a new social setting and to receive tools to fully integrate them within that system. This city center fills typical recreation center needs but also provides services relating to employment, housing, consumer protection, welfare, health, office, day care, senior issues, and other programs. A branch library is on site, and a farmers market takes place on Tuesday. Also on site is the public art *Homage to Quetzalcoatl.* (Both, Espinoza Collection.)

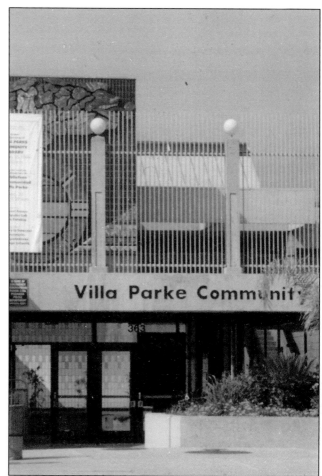

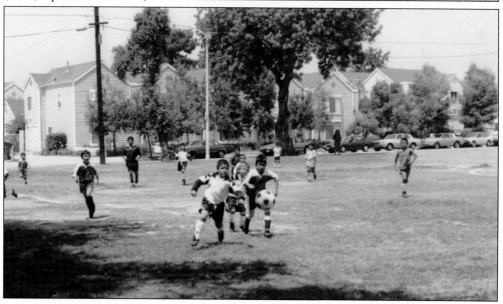

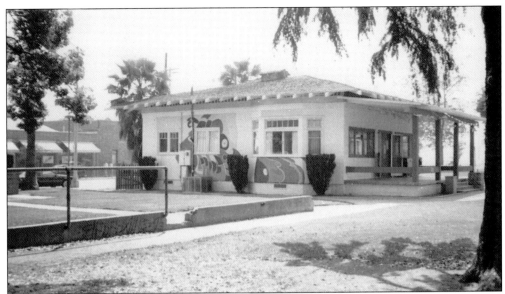

El Centro de Información, later the El Centro de Acción Social, developed out of the political empowerment that was prevalent in the Chicano community in Pasadena. When it was established in 1968, it provided services to the Latino community, which then made up 10 percent of the population of the city of Pasadena. Its advocacy was strengthened by collaborative efforts of individuals involved with the city, the schools, and the community. (Latino Heritage Collection.)

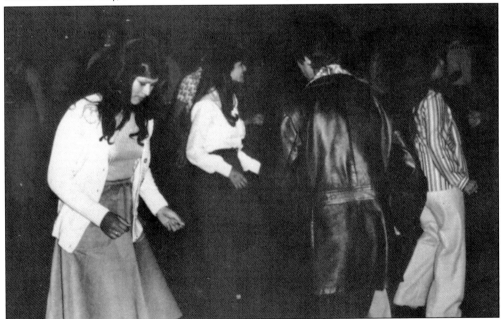

In this period in Pasadena, there was a Movimiento Estudiantil Chicano de Aztlan (MEChA) group at each of the high schools, one at Pasadena City College, and a formalized MEChA council. Unique to Pasadena, the MEChA at John Muir High School's Cinco de Mayo event was complete with queen and court. As the group's president, Rosemary Reyna led a student organization, which was pivotal to the implementation of Chicano studies in Pasadena. (Pasadena Unified School Collection.)

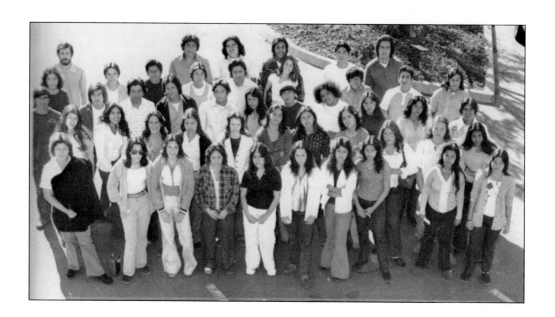

Throughout most of the 20th century, the vast majority of Latinos living in Pasadena were of Mexican ancestry and descent. They and their parents had lived in the United States for generations. In the early 1970s, there was an increase in those whose families had more recently come from Mexico and many from Central and Latin America. The two groups at Blair High School pictured here in 1976 are a visual testament to the changes taking place. The text accompanying the photographs reinforces this difference in focus. The Latin-American Student Association (LASA, above) was composed of students from many parts of Latin America "working together to bring cultural unity among its members, and to enlighten other students about Latin-American cultures." The purpose of the MEChA club (below) was "to improve the educational system in Pasadena by requesting from school reform in regards to Mexicans and other Latin-American people." (Above, Pasadena Unified School District; below, Pasadena Unified School District.)

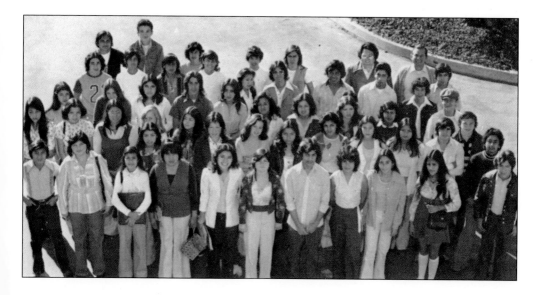

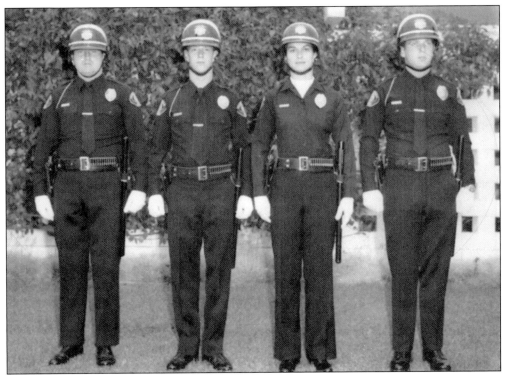

In 1974, Marilyn Diaz, second from right, became a pioneer in the Pasadena Police Department. Other women were in the department, but she was the first to be directly appointed to patrol. She and her superiors deliberated on her uniform; a white turtleneck was added to make her uniform more feminine. In 2006, she became chief of police of Sierra Madre, the first female police chief in the county and the 12th in California. (Pasadena Police Department.)

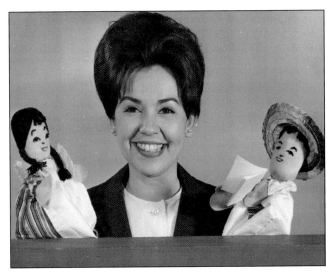

Yvette Lightfoot, of Puerto Rican heritage, was one of few Latinos working for Pasadena Unified School District (PUSD) in the early 1960s. She oversaw a new program, foreign language instruction at the elementary level, which led to a television series for the California State Department of Education. She also was in charge of intergroup education. This picture of her belies her involvement and commitment to change for Latino students in PUSD. (Pasadena Museum of History.)

Following the rise of Fidel Castro in 1959, many professionals left Cuba, the majority landing in Florida. Relocation programs developed by governmental and religious groups brought families to the Pasadena area. They developed social clubs and a Cuban Little League team and had fund-raising dances where the señoras contributed their cooking. Oscar Palmer (top, right-hand column) was among those who became a part of Pasadena, retiring as principal of Rose City High School. (Pasadena Unified School District.)

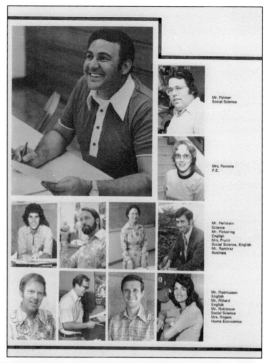

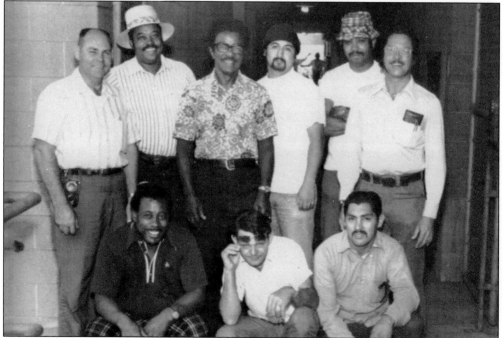

This 1976 picture of custodians at Blair High School reflects the changing styles and attitudes that were taking place throughout the school community. Many, if not most, of the custodians had lived the bulk of their lives in Pasadena. Identified only by last name, from left to right, are (first row) Hallie, Gutierrez, and Buelna; (second row) Burr, Adams, Clark, Cervara, Dunn, and Dixon. (Pasadena Museum of History.)

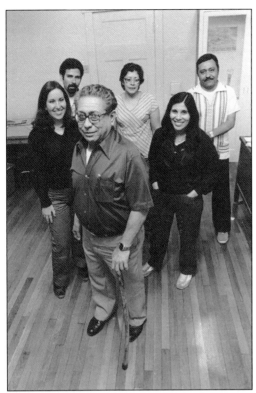

Emilio "Hip" Cervera became active in the Chicano movement in Pasadena when his children were in high school. His involvement bridged the efforts of Stephen Reyes, Trinidad de Caro, Maxine Casso, Phil Gutierrez, and the younger community. As director of El Centro, Cervera is front and center, and with him, from left to right, are Kim Resendiz, Nicholas Rodriguez, Dolores Ibarra, Jorge Oliva and future El Centro director Leonora Barron. (Espinosa Collection.)

Ramon C. Cortines was Pasadena Unified School District superintendent from 1972 through 1978 and again from 1979 to 1984. Serving during a most turbulent time in education in the district, at a time when policy and politics were incredibly personal, Cortines showed an unwavering commitment to the education of children throughout the district. He is pictured here with Sophie Monteroro at the Wilson Junior High graduation in June 1982. (Pasadena Unified School District.)

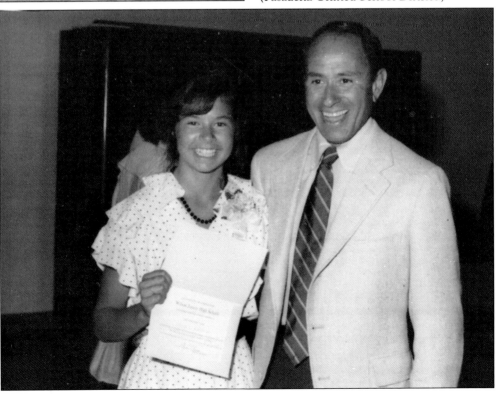

In February 1979, Harold N. Hubbard's lead to his story in the *Star News* was, "We must be ruled by reason not sentiment," one view of the controversy over whether to rebuild the burned Guadalupe church in Pasadena. "We are fighting for our church with our hearts—and we will not stop," is the other view. The church is pictured here before the fire. It was not rebuilt. (Pasadena Museum of History.)

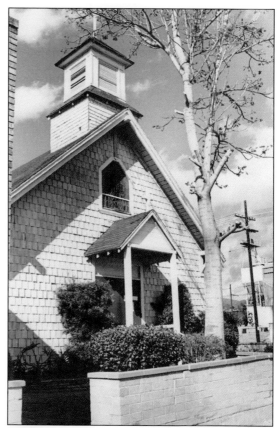

Yuny Parada was born in El Salvador. She completed her bachelor's degree as the economy was collapsing from a civil war in which as many as 70,000 people died. In San Salvador, she met a "long lost" aunt who brought her to Los Angeles. Upon her arrival, she attended school nine hours a day to learn English. She is pictured at her job at a Japanese Trading Center in 1978. (Parada Collection.)

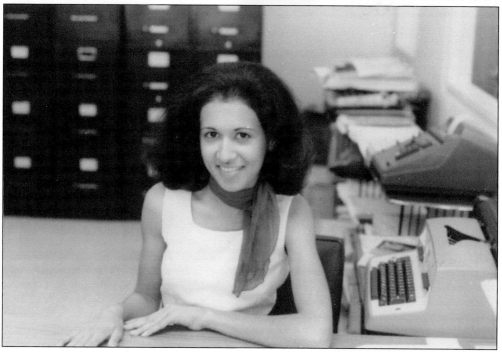

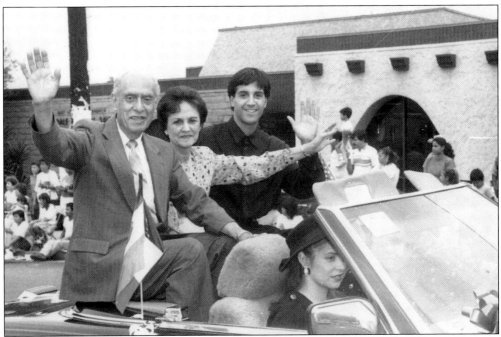

Ed Roybal (seated left) was elected to Los Angeles City Council. In 1962, he was the first Hispanic elected from California to the U.S. Congress in the 20th century. He authored the first bilingual education bill and sponsored legislation to establish National Hispanic Week, a precursor to Hispanic Heritage Month. While representing California's 25th Congressional District, including Pasadena, he cofounded the Congressional Hispanic Caucus and the National Association of Latino Elected Officials. (Roybal Collection.)

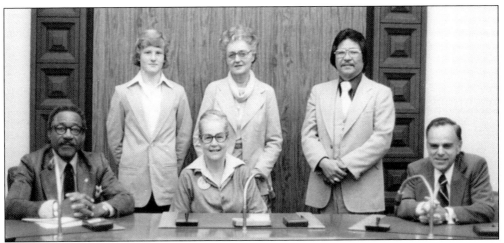

Filemon "Phil" Gutierrez (standing, far right) heard stories from members of the community while they sat in his barber's chair. This led him to ardently advocate for the Chicano community. When a school board member resigned, Gutierrez was appointed in a motion led by members Elbie Hickambottom and Marge Wyatt. Knowing he had been active at El Centro, they believed he would share information regarding the needs of students from his community. (Pasadena Unified School District.)

Nine

NEW VOICES, NEW REALITIES

The number of Latinos in Pasadena continued to grow: from nearly 30 percent in 1990 to approximately 35 percent in 2000. For the first century of Pasadena's existence, the predominant group of Latinos had been those of Mexican heritage. During the 1980s, population representing this growth had become more diverse. During the 30 years that followed World War II, the long-standing communities that had been a part of Pasadena history declined. Simultaneous with the decline of the old center of the city and then the development of Old Pasadena, with restaurants and hotels, the Latino population began to migrate to the area of affordable housing north of the 210 Freeway. Antipathy that had been a part of earlier interactions between native-born and immigrant communities experienced resurgence, including native-born Latinos. Immigrants without papers became "Illegals," an adjective that became used as noun to describe the group and its individuals. The word Chicano also became a point of argument. To many who had lived in the United States, the word symbolized the experience of one who has been oppressed and is of Hispanic heritage. To many immigrants, this was a word with meaning only to Mexican Americans. In the early part of the 20th century, groups were predominantly affiliated with church or fraternity. With the increase in the number of Latinos gaining greater education came an increase in those who became affiliated with organizing, political and professional entities. Groups like Latinos for Economic Advancement and Development; IMPACTO, a political action group; Vecinos Unidos; Club Latino at Cal Tech; and Amigos Unidos at Jet Propulsion Laboratory were established during this period.

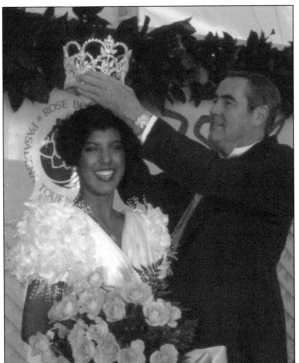

The 1993 Tournament of Roses sets a new milestone with the appointment of the 75th Rose Queen, Liana Carisa Yamasaki. Queen Liana was senior at Alverno High School and worked on the student-run television station and student-run government, where she served as the chief justice of the Supreme Court. The Temple City resident of Japanese, Chinese, and Peruvian heritage is the daughter of Elena and Jose Yamasaki. (Pasadena Tournament of Roses Archive.)

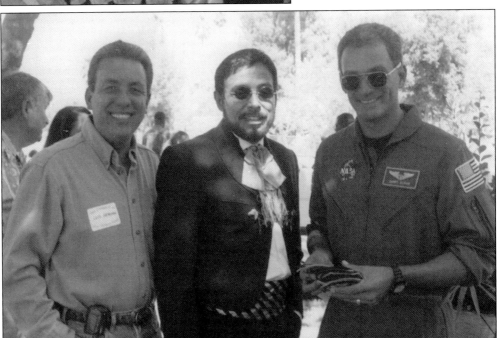

Millions are familiar with the work of Raul Rodriguez, seen here with Pasadena Information Services officer Luis Herrera and astronaut Daniel J. Olivas. Every year, Raul rides on a float that he designed for the Tournament of Roses Parade. At age 15, he designed the City of Whittier float for the parade. He has won more awards than any other designer in the history of the event. (Latino Heritage Collection.)

Jesucita Hernandez grew tobacco with her family in Jalisco, Mexico. She lived through tumultuous personal and political times and arrived in Pasadena a widow with children. She began to make tortillas and tamales, opened a boardinghouse, and married Antonio Mijares. As life became less turbulent, business flourished. A proud, smart businesswoman, she leveraged a loan to build Mijares Restaurant and, after it was destroyed by fire, rebuilt the restaurant. (Mijares Collection.)

In 1977, the City of Pasadena subsidized the building of 50 townhouses. To qualify, there was a maximum annual income and a required $2,000 as deposit to be entered into the "lottery." Yuny Parada and her husband, Ranjit Vishwanath, moved into their first Pasadena home for $54,000. Four years later, she and her family left. She felt it was important for her children to connect with nature by having ducks, which was not permitted. (Parada Collection.)

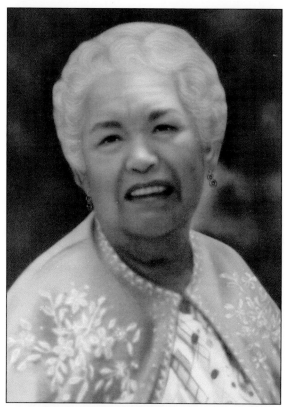

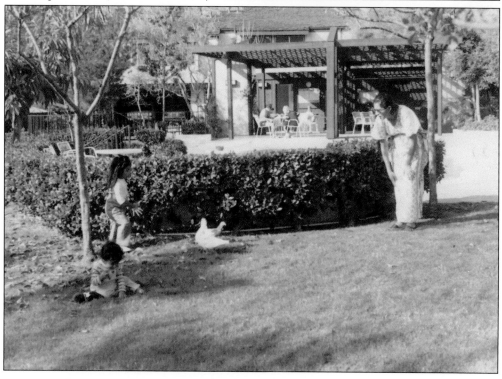

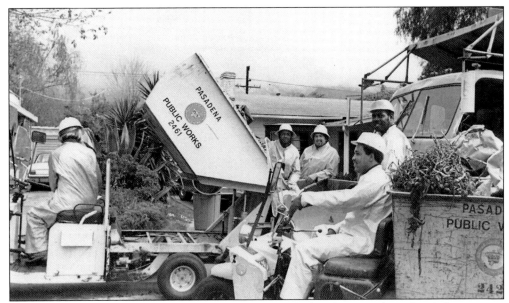

During the 1980s and 1990s, many of the people who worked in the City of Pasadena's departments had grown up in the city. They showed great pride in the work they did for the city in part because it had been their home and the home of their parents. With rising costs of homes, the numbers of city workers who could live in the city began to decrease. (Pasadena Public Library.)

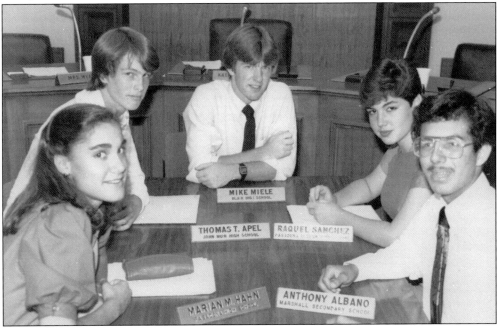

Raquel Sanchez is apparently a student board member representing Pasadena Alternative School in 1983. PAS began at Washington Elementary and became a cooperative venture of University of Massachusetts and the district. At one point, it was renamed Washington Center for Alternative Studies, and an evening high school was started at the same site. The school moved to Hale Elementary School in 1996, eventually being named Norma Coombs Alternative School. (Pasadena Unified School District.)

Fourth-grader Daisy Chilin was at Longfellow Elementary School in November 1992 when she entered an essay contest. Daisy wrote that she liked the Pilgrims because they represented religious freedom and liberty. She didn't share that she more closely identified with her indigenous roots. There were two essay winners who shared the costume for the day. Daisy wore the costume in the afternoon when this picture was taken. (Chilin Collection.)

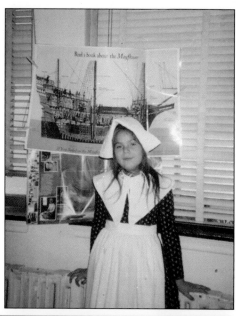

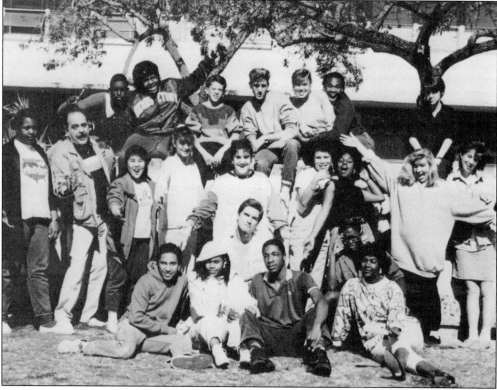

Abel Franco (second from left) taught in the Pasadena Unified School District for 30 years. He was a working actor and a producer and was among the first who practiced "color blind" casting: choosing actors without regard to their ethnicity or race. He taught thousands of students and is remembered fondly. The Abel Franco Theater at Pasadena High School honors the memory of his work and his impact on the lives of the students he taught. (Pasadena Unified School District.)

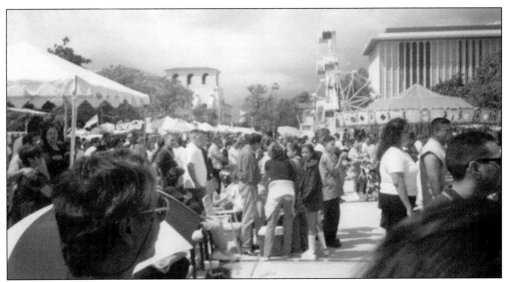

The Pasadena Latino Employees Association began as a voice for city employees of Latin American descent. Among its primary goals has been the improvement of opportunities for career enhancement, to market city services to the Latino community in Pasadena, and to promote and assist inter-group communication and cooperation. It has worked in collaboration with the Cinco de Mayo Committee to support the Cinco de Mayo Celebration, pictured here. (Monzon Collection.)

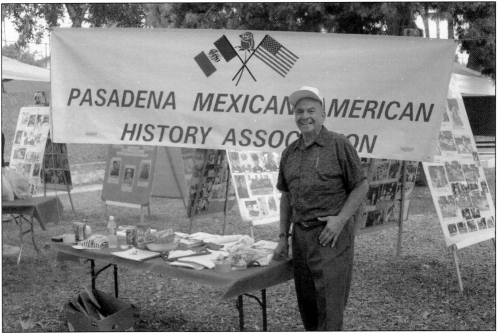

The Pasadena Mexican American History Association members are seniors whose expressed desire and work is to save the history of this community; without their work, the fullness of Mexican American history in Pasadena would have become lost. They generously share their life stories and pictures with many other groups in the area so that all may learn this part of Pasadena's history. (Pasadena Mexican American History Association.)

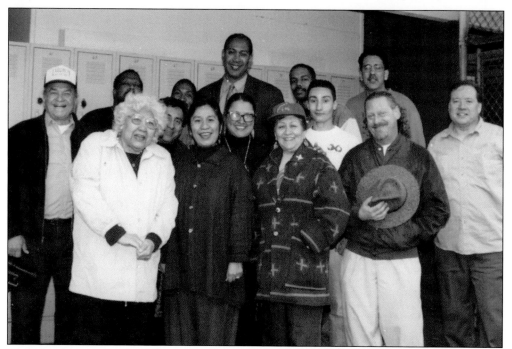

The idea for a Latino parade occurred to Roberta Martínez while viewing an Irish parade in Pasadena. Working with her codirector of the Latino Cultural Academy, Sandi Romero, with the encouragement from council member Bill Crowfoot, a new tradition began. The first attempt was rained out; council member Chris Holden (back row, center) is in this group photograph. The committee regrouped, and the parade took place six months later. (Latino Heritage Collection.)

The post-parade event was called a *jamaica* because it recalled the celebrations that had taken place at Our Lady of Guadalupe. Students from Pasadena high schools are docents of the historic photograph exhibit at the *jamaica*. Learning the history of those who came before and sharing this knowledge highlights experiences and role models of the Latinos who have been a part of the city since before its formal establishment.

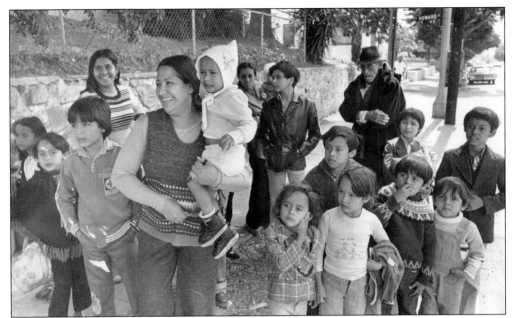

Attribution text for this 1981 photograph includes, "Jose Castillo's family from El Salvador waits at a . . . bus stop at Fair Oaks and Howard Street after being released from a detention center." It is estimated that nearly one-third of the workforce left El Salvador because of the civil war. Some refugees remained in countries of refuge; others returned home, as early as 1987, to rebuild their country. (Security Pacific Collection/Los Angeles Public Library.)

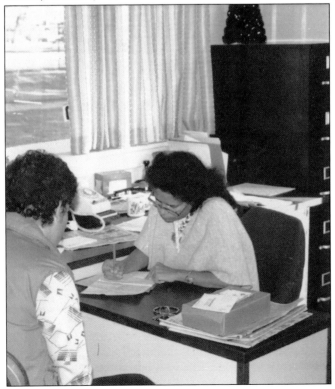

Over time, the agency El Centro de Información had become El Centro de Acción Social. Among the services provided by El Centro were referrals for community members who needed help with a social system that was complicated and unfamiliar to them. Juanita Espino at El Centro, and others working at Villa Parke, provided help for all community members needing advocacy and guidance. (Espino Collection.)

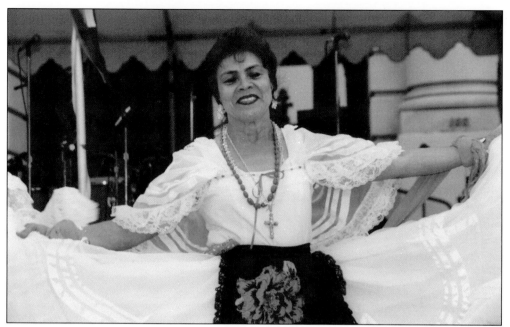

Lupe Reyes, Grupo Sabor de Mexico, has been performing longest, beginning as a member of the Valadez Sisters in the 1950s. *Maestra* Rosalina Guerrero, with Grupo Sonrisa at Sacred Heart Church, was drawn to folklorico because of the complexity of construction and design worn in traditional folklorico costumes. Folklorico groups led by Rosie Cortez, Juan Espino, Fatima Mendoza, and Gabriela De Leon keep the folklorico tradition alive in Pasadena. (Guerrero Collection.)

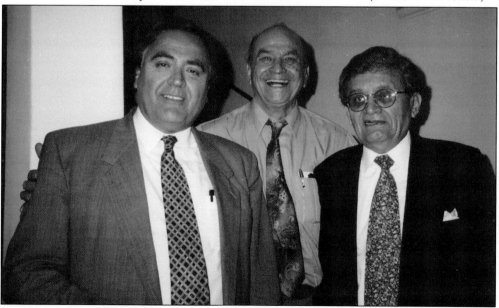

In 1992, George Padilla (far left) became the first elected Latino to the Pasadena Unified School Board, serving as board president from 1995 to 1997. He was among the leaders for Measure Y passage and advocated for the needs of Latino students, then 40 percent of the district. Beside Padilla is Manny Contreras and Phil Montes, former director of the Association of Mexican American Educators. (Manuel Contreras Collection.)

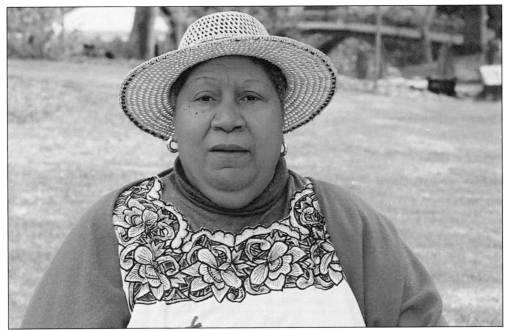

As a young person, Romelia Kirkaldy lived in Colón, Panama Canal Zone. Her father worked for the U.S. government. She remembers occasionally being treated with some reserve when some acquaintances learned of her father's employer. Following her parents' death in 1989, she moved to Pasadena at the invitation of a niece attending school in the area. Romelia worked at the nursery at the Huntington Hospital. (Monzon Collection.)

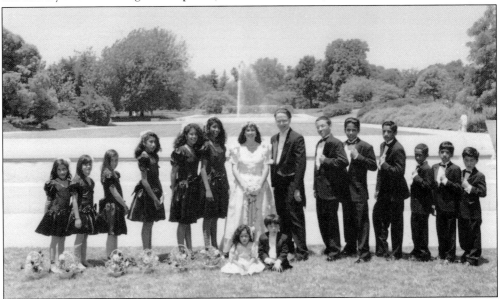

La quinceañera, celebrating a young woman's 15th birthday, had become a rarity in Pasadena by the mid-20th century. Increasing numbers of Latinos living in Pasadena helped revive the practice. Sindy Guevara's *quinceañera* included cousins Anita, Reena, and Raul Vishnawath, whose mother was from El Salvador and father from India. The photographs were taken at the Arboretum, followed by a reception at the Parada Vishwanath home in Chapman Woods. (Parada Collection.)

116

Lalo Guerrero was known as the "Father of Chicano Music." He wrote about what he saw and documented the Mexican American, Chicano, and Latino experience in the United States. Committed to supporting efforts at strengthening the Chicano/Latino community, he donated his time and musical talents. Papa Lalo was an honoree at the Chicano Music Awards and the first grand marshal of the Latino History parade and *jamaica*. (Daniel and Stella Collection.)

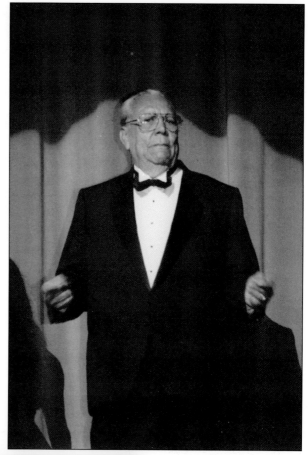

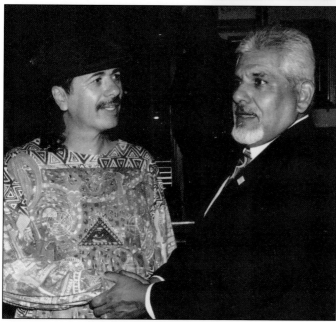

Daniel Castro has contributed to his community in unique ways. His radio broadcast, *Sancho Show*, encouraged youth to stay and advance in school. It functioned as an on-air community center, offering local information and a calendar of events between music segments. At the Chicano Music Awards, recipients of the Quetzalcoatl Memorial Scholarship shared the stage with luminaries like Carlos Santana who donated their time and talents to raise money for scholarships. (Collection of Daniel and Stella Castro.)

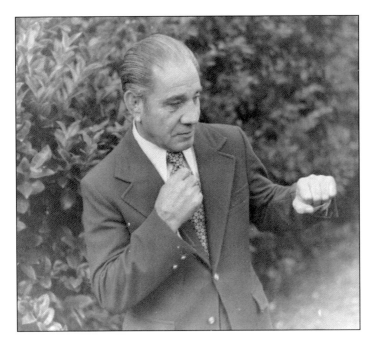

On July 16, 1932, Canto Robledo won the Pacific Bantamweight Championship. After he became blind as a result of injuries in the ring, he trained thousands of fighters. Hand on shoulder, he would tell the fighter to throw a set of combinations and then tell them corrections to be made. Canto received his Championship Belt as the Joe Louis Humanitarian Memorial Award in November 1988. (Robledo Collection.)

The mission of the Pasadena Latino Forum is to convene community groups and their members in order to advocate for equity of the Pasadena Latino community. It presents comments and concerns shared with them to the larger institutions of the city. Pictured here are board members Yuny Parada, cochair Robert Monzón, Roberta Martínez, Felipe Infante, cochair Inez Yslas, Susana Zamorando, Mario Maytorena, and Daisy Chilin. (Monzon Collection.)

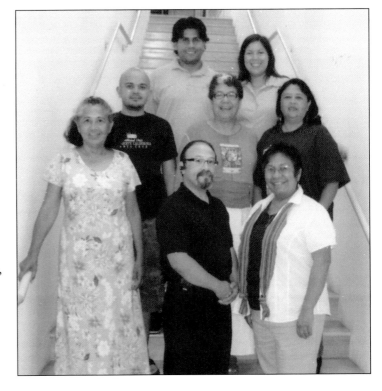

118

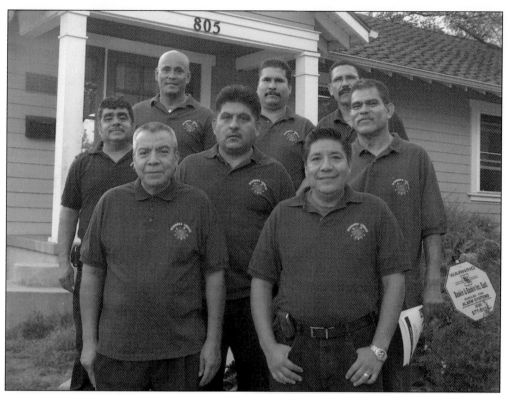

Hombres Unidos meet weekly at Madison Elementary School, where 80 percent of the school population is Latino, and the majority of students have Spanish as their primary language. These neighbors are committed to helping young people and families lead happy and healthy lives. They sponsor trainings and events in areas such as leadership development, computers and technology, community safety, vocational skill building, financial management, health education, and parenting. (Madison Neighborhood Partners.)

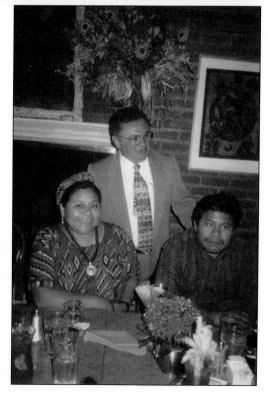

Rigoberta Menchu Tum won the Nobel Peace Prize in 1992 for her dedication to publicizing the plight of Guatemala's indigenous peoples. To further her work, a foundation was established. A fund-raiser to support this work took place at Villa Parke hosted by the Latino Cultural Academy. Following a successful fund-raiser, Tum and her husband, Angel Canil (both seated), enjoyed dinner hosted by Abel Ramirez of El Portal Restaurant. (Isenberg Collection.)

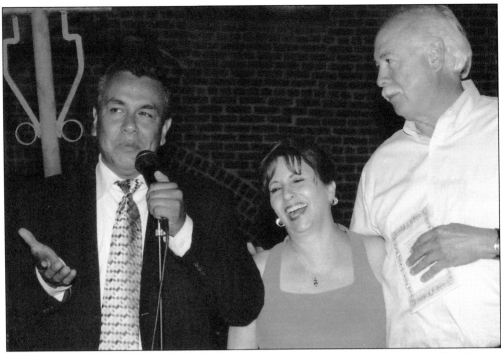

La Raza Association faculty and staff members are, from left to right, James Aragon, Alice Castro Araiza, and Arnolfo Ramirez. They express comments and concerns regarding the hiring and retention of Latino faculty and staff. The group has established scholarships that are used by transfer students to four-year colleges and universities. Working with counselors from the Puente Program, they award scholarships at an annual luncheon. (La Raza Collection.)

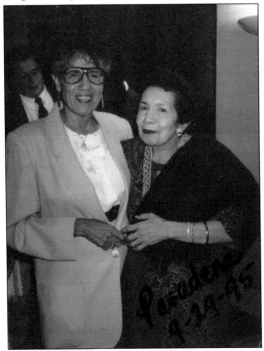

Marina Rodriguez and Jesse Magdaleno Lopez are among the seniors in our community who have lived the through challenging times. Each had their own way of moving forward. Marina, on the left, who has been a photographer, musician, and bullfighter, moved ahead with her determination and talent, a role model for those around her; Jesse worked for years informally as a grassroots organizer. Each woman gave of her talents in her own way. (Manuel Contreras Collection.)

Ten

FROM THEN TO NOW

For nearly 200 years, Latinos have worked and lived in the northernmost part of the San Gabriel Valley, in the area that is Pasadena. The experiences and history of the earliest settlers were shared in short sentences and phrases inserted in letters and memoirs. The community histories can be found in newspaper and magazine headlines. The lives of those who lived in the early 20th century can be found in the stories shared by seniors still here to share them. Some of the topics of the last century continue to return; affordable housing, business opportunities, economic viability, educational achievement, and incorporation into the mainstream society while retaining cultural sensibilities will likely be a part of the balancing act between city and citizen. The tenor toward immigrants, feelings of displacement in the job market, and the global economy will likely continue to inform political and social choices. Until the year 2000, there had been a total of three Latinos who had served on either city council or the school board. In 2001, Victor M. Gordo de Arteaga, Esteban "Steve" Lizardo, and Dr. Consuelo Rey Castro were elected to office. Gordo, who was elected to the Pasadena City Council, had served as District 5 field representative to then vice mayor Bill Crowfoot. Lizardo, who is a labor lawyer, was elected to the Pasadena Unified School Board. Castro is a political science professor and has served as a union chief negotiator for the Los Angeles Community College District; she was elected to the Pasadena City College Board of Trustees. In 2007, Edwin Diaz became superintendent of Pasadena Unified School District and Dr. Paulette J. Perfumo became president of Pasadena City College. What these leaders and community members, Latino and non-Latino, find as common ground for working together will establish the future of Latinos in Pasadena.

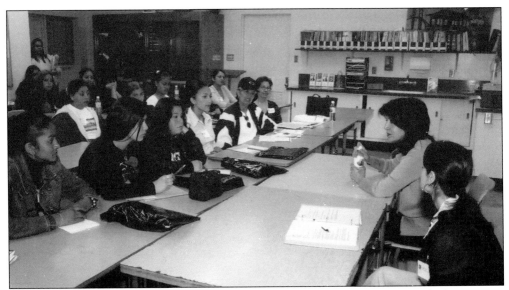

In response to the problems facing young Latinas, Adelante Mujer Latina, a daylong career conference program, was established. Originally hosted by Women At Work and currently hosted by the Pasadena Youth Center, the program brings together more than 1,500 Latinas ages 14 to 21 with their mentors or mothers to attend interactive workshops like this one led by Evelina Fernandez. It is the largest gathering of Latinas in the state. (Adelante Mujer Latina Collection.)

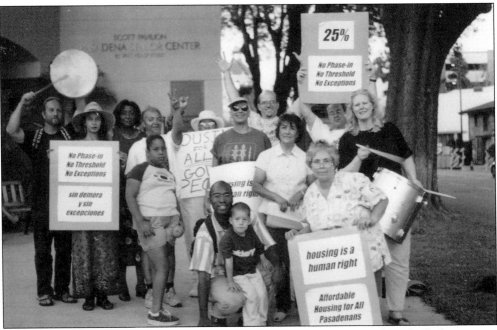

Herminia Ortiz arrived in Pasadena as an undocumented immigrant and gradually became an active advocate for the immigrant community. She works with others in her neighborhood to find solutions for issues of concern in the city or schools. She is in this group photograph (to the left of the drummer) protesting the lack of affordable housing in the city. Despite being a monolingual Spanish speaker, she ran for city council in 2005. (Ortiz Collection.)

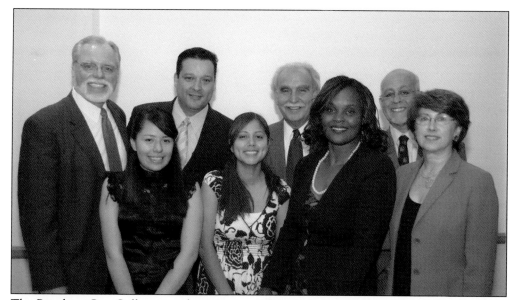

The Pasadena City College president's Latino Advisory Committee focuses on enhancing the educational successes of Latino Students at PCC. A scholarship subcommittee was formed in 2003 charged with providing scholarships for students attending PCC. Pictured here are student recipient and cochair Lola Proaño-Gomez (front, far right), former PCC president James P. Kossler, council member Victor Gordo, advisory committee cochairs, Armando Gonzalez, and Hank Guerrero. (Pasadena City College Collection.)

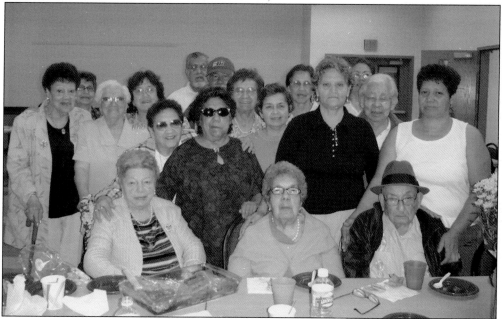

The Latino Club at the Pasadena Senior Center is pictured here celebrating the 104th birthday of Don Margarito Montaño in 2006. His wife, Baudelia Montaño, a youthful 96 years old, is seated beside him. Both were born in Jalisco, Mexico, and they were married for over 70 years. They lived most of their lives in Pasadena. Don Margarito passed away in 2006, and his wife passed away one year later. (Pasadena Senior Center.)

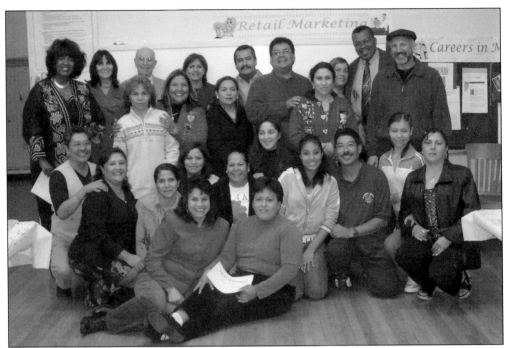

IDEPSCA and APPLE work with the immigrant community in the Pasadena area. Through leadership development and educational programs based in popular education methodology, they focus on issues particular to the immigrant experience and work to develop leadership skills for parent participants via the parent organization. Esteban Lizardo, in the back row wearing glasses, a current member and former president of the Pasadena Unified School District, is pictured with them. (APPLE/IDEPSCA Collection.)

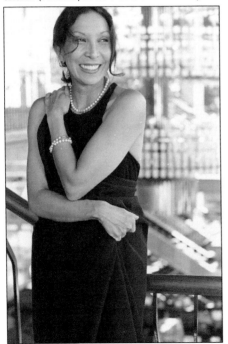

International opera diva Suzanna Guzmán has deep roots in Pasadena. Her father was born on Peach Street, and her first rehearsals were in a rock band across from Central Park. Her vocal therapist tricked her into an opera audition; she was cast as Carmen. She has sung with opera legends, performed in great opera houses, been a radio broadcaster, and created her one-woman show, *Don't Be Afraid! It's Just Opera.* (Humphrey.)

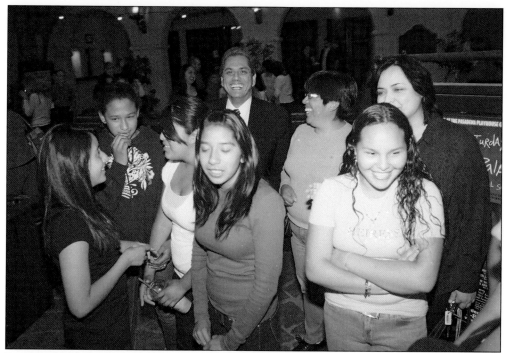

Pasadena Unified School District superintendent Edwin Diaz was born in Gilroy and was among the first in his family to attend college. He was superintendent of the Gilroy Unified School District. Superintendent Diaz is challenged in Pasadena by a legacy fraught with political contention regarding educational curriculum, issues of equity, and declining student enrollment. He shares a moment of levity with students at a performance at the Pasadena Playhouse. (Pasadena Latino Forum Collection.)

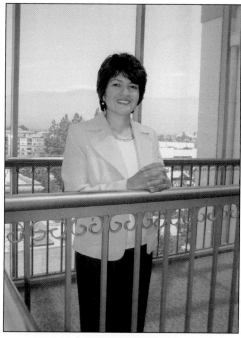

Pasadena assistant city manager Julie Gutierrez is a third-generation Pasadenan. She took college preparatory in high school despite her counselor advising her to take vocational courses. She graduated from Pomona College with a bachelor's degree in theater administration and from University of LaVerne with a master's degree in business administration. She is currently responsible for tracking legislative issues and acts as liaison for seven city departments. (City of Pasadena.)

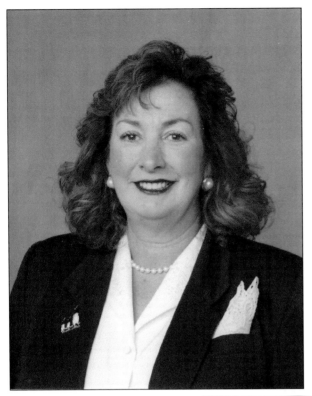

Pasadena City College president Dr. Paulette J. Perfumo has been a part of the California Community Colleges system for some time. She has served the California campuses of Solano Community College, Ohlone College, and Lassen Community College. Dr. Perfumo began her college teaching career at College of the Canyons in 1978. Perfumo holds a bachelor of science degree from Oregon State University and a master's degree and Ph.D. from UCLA. (Pasadena City College Collection.)

Dr. Consuelo Rey Castro has lived her life in the possible. She attended Santa Barbara City College and completed her bachelor's and master's degrees at Loyola University. Dr. Rey Castro has encouraged students of all ages to fulfill their aspirations. She earned her doctorate from the University of Southern California while teaching at East Los Angeles College and serving on the Pasadena City College Board of Trustees. (Pasadena City College Collection.)

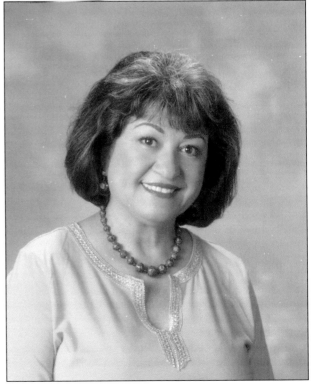

This picture was taken at Pasadena City Hall during the World Cup in 1994. Manny Contreras, a guardian of history, captured a bit of history with this image, which is special to him because it combines the mariachis, symbolizing his ancestry, the city he loves, and the life he has lived. (Contreras Collection.)

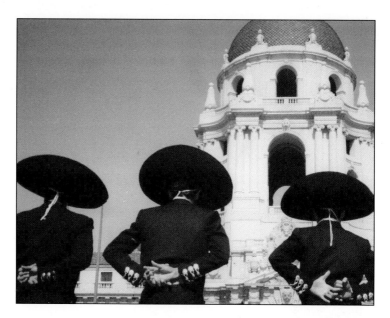

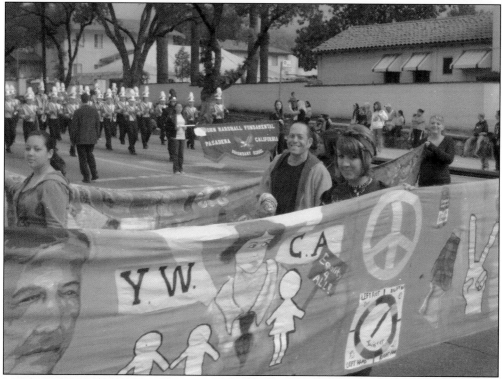

Members of the Marshall High School Band and the Pasadena High School Visual Arts and Design Academy are citizens of the cities that make up much of what was Rancho San Pascual. Their education in the arts, history, math, science, and vocational trades and their active participation in the administration and governance of Pasadena will help define the next chapters of the history of Latinos in Pasadena.

DISCOVER THOUSANDS OF LOCAL HISTORY BOOKS
FEATURING MILLIONS OF VINTAGE IMAGES

Arcadia Publishing, the leading local history publisher in the United States, is committed to making history accessible and meaningful through publishing books that celebrate and preserve the heritage of America's people and places.

Find more books like this at
www.arcadiapublishing.com

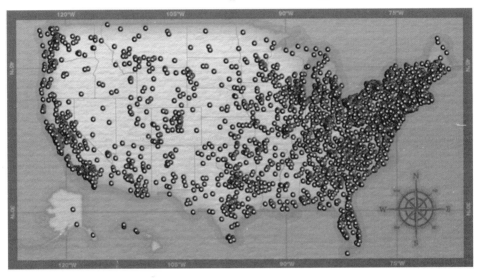

Search for your hometown history, your old stomping grounds, and even your favorite sports team.

Consistent with our mission to preserve history on a local level, this book was printed in South Carolina on American-made paper and manufactured entirely in the United States. Products carrying the accredited Forest Stewardship Council (FSC) label are printed on 100 percent FSC-certified paper.

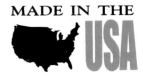

MADE IN THE
USA